BIRTH OF THE COMMUNIST MANIFESTO

D0901147

Karl Marx in 1848

Frederick Engels in the 1840's

Birth
of the
Communist
Manifesto

With Full Text of the *Manifesto*, all Prefaces by
Marx and Engels, Early Drafts by Engels and
other Supplementary Material

Edited and Annotated, with an Introduction

by DIRK J. STRUIK

 INTERNATIONAL PUBLISHERS *New York*

Library of Congress Catalog Card Number: 77-148513
SBN 7178–0288–4 (cloth) ; 7178–0320–1 (paperback)
Printed in the United States of America

OCLC

To the memory of

ALEXANDER TRACHTENBERG

EDITOR'S NOTE

This edition of the *Communist Manifesto* together with documents relating to it is preceded by a historical introduction sketching the social and intellectual climate in which it was conceived. Stress is laid on the motives which guided its authors and the reasons for its lasting importance. New is the section on the early history of the *Manifesto* in the United States and the incorporation of some of the material recently discovered on the League of the Just, including a translation of a newly found Credo of Engels. Where the translation of the original German was made by or under the supervision of Engels it has, of course, been left intact; otherwise the translation is the editor's or is based on an existing one and checked against the original.

Special thanks for encouragement, advice and other help go to James S. Allen, Horace Davis, John Kykiri, Boone Schirmer and Ruth Struik.

Belmont, Mass.
January 1971

DIRK J. STRUIK

CONTENTS

PART ONE

INTRODUCTION

BIRTH OF THE COMMUNIST MANIFESTO AND ITS HISTORICAL SIGNIFICANCE

by DIRK J. STRUIK

Revolt of the Silesian weavers, 1844. *Etching by Kate Kollwitz.*

I. THE DOUBLE REVOLUTION

> We hold these truths to be self-evident, that all men are created equal, that they are endowed by their Creator with certain inalienable Rights, that among these are Life, Liberty and the pursuit of Happiness.
> —*Declaration of Independence, 1776*

> Every political association has as its goal the preservation of the natural and inprescriptible rights of men. These rights are liberty, property, security and resistance to oppression.
> —Art. 11, *Declaration of Rights of Man and the Citizen, 1789*

1.

The *Communist Manifesto* is the most famous of all socialist documents. It appeared in February 1848, on the eve of the European revolution the authors had foreseen. They were still young men, not yet 30 years of age, but already mature in experience, acquired in several years of passionate engagement in the political struggles of their time. Starting as radical democrats, fighters for constitutional rights in Germany, and especially for freedom of the press, popular representation and abolition of feudal privileges, Marx and Engels had developed into militant socialists, or communists, as they called themselves. At the same time they were social scientists with an extraordinary grasp of the political and economic conditions of their age, a grasp already displayed in newspaper articles, in essays and even books. The *Communist Manifesto* summarized their conclusions in a style as brilliant as it is succinct. Although it is more than 120 years old, it is as invigorating and topical as on the day it was written.

The *Manifesto* represents a landmark in the history of thought and especially of socialist thought. Socialism, before Marx and Engels, flourished in dozens of different schools and sects, a conglomeration of brilliant insights, hopeful wishes, militant exclamations and daring deeds. It was incoherent, its course like that of a ship blown over the waters by winds from all sides, unable to set its own direction. What Marx and Engels did was to seek out the sound elements in the many theories, testing their findings against the best of contemporary philosophical and scientific thought and against the accumulated practice of revolutionary struggles. They integrated their discoveries into a new and vital socialist world outlook. As with every great theory, that of Marx and Engels originated as a creative synthesis of scattered facts and doctrines, many already known, but now illuminated by new and deeper insight. Thus Marx and Engels lifted socialism from the realm of utopia to the realm of science.

This synthesis was brought into being between 1843 and 1845. In the following three years Marx and Engels sought further self-clarification, testing their ideas in the political struggle and in the study of history and economics. Their conclusions proved so trenchant, even prophetic, and were presented so vividly in the *Communist Manifesto* that it is the only one of the many socialist "manifestoes" and "credos" of those revolutionary days which has survived as a living document. All the others, in so far as they have been preserved at all, are gathering dust in the archives, some occasionally resuscitated as a curiosity.

To understand how the *Communist Manifesto* came to be written, we must go back half a century into history.

2.

For 50 years the world, the Atlantic world, at any rate, had been in revolutionary turmoil. A double revolution was going on. Looming large in the recent past was the great French Revolution of 1789, never forgotten and still raising hopes and fears. Besides this primarily political Revolution, stood the British Industrial Revolution, under way since about 1770, and slowly creeping across the Atlantic and the North Sea. Of the two, the French Revolution had been by all odds the more spectacular. For Europeans of the early half of the 19th century it was *the* Revolution. True, the American Revolution preceded and in part inspired it. The influence of the American Revolution, however, was most directly felt in the western hemisphere, where it prepared the way for the industrial revolution in the United States and was a precedent for the independence movement in Latin America. It was the French Revolution that shook the whole of Europe with an impact felt to this very day.

The French Revolution is one of the most dramatic events in history. It swept away all feudal encumbrances impeding the development of capitalism and bourgeois society. At its most crucial moments, as in 1792 when foreign armies invaded France, it brought the masses of the people into decisive and often violent action. But the fruits were eventually harvested by the bourgeoisie, that is, by the nascent industrial middle class and those financial and commercial circles opposed to the nobility and to feudal privileges in general, the so-called *Tiers État,* the third estate. For the first time in history this bourgeoisie became the sole ruling class in a great country. Marx expressed it in his pithy manner:

In 1789 the bourgeoisie was allied with the people against the monarchy, the nobility and the ruling church. The bourgeoisie was the class that *in reality* stood at the head of the movement. The proletariat and those sections of the civil population not belonging to the bourgeoisie either had not yet any interests different from those of the bourgeoisie, or did not yet constitute independently developed classes or sections of classes. When therefore they acted against the bourgeoisie, as for instance during 1793–94 in France*, they fought only to achieve the goals of the bourgeoisie, though not in the manner of the bourgeoisie. The whole French terror was nothing but a plebeian way to dispose of the enemies of the bourgeoisie: absolutism, feudalism and their narrow-minded civilian associates *(Spieszbürgertum).*[1]

---

* This was the period of the Terror, in which political power was for a while in the hands of the Paris radical democrats, composed mainly of mechanics, artisans and small traders. The leadership in that period was exercised by Robespierre and the Jacobins.

Yet, as Marx continued, the victory of this middle class was at that time a *victory of a new order of society:* the victory of bourgeois over feudal property, of the national over the provincial idea, of competition over guild association, of the division of the landed estates over entail, of enlightenment over superstition, of industry over heroic laziness, of bourgeois law over medieval privileges—most of which victories, we should add, were already taken for granted in the United States. Marx thus stressed the progressive character of the revolution, with the bourgeoisie acting as the representative of the whole of society against the outdated classes, the nobility and higher clergy, and hence at that period also acting for the still insufficiently developed working class.

Two legal landmarks of the French Revolution remained vividly in the memory of man: the Constitution of 1791 and the Constitution of 1793. They were accompanied by a *Declaration of the Rights of Man and the Citizen,* inspired by the doctrines of the Enlightenment (Locke, Rousseau) as well as by the American Constitution and the Declaration of Independence. France under the Bourbon kings had been an absolute monarchy. Now the radical break had come. The Constitution of 1791 established a constitutional monarchy and a moderately liberal regime dominated by the upper middle class (with some enlightened aristocrats, such as Mirabeau). The Constitution of 1793 established a democratic republic "one and indivisible," based on a very broad electorate and intensive participation by the masses of the population. This first democratic constitution of modern times, more advanced than the American one of 1789 (which, among other things, did not abolish slavery) remained the political ideal of radical democrats, though by 1794 it passed into history with the fall of Robespierre. The ensuing Directory drafted a new, less democratic, constitution.

Under the banner of radical democracy the French Revolution sent its *sans-culotte* armies across the borders of France, proclaiming liberty, equality and fraternity. *Guerre aux palais, paix aux cabanes!*—war on the palaces, peace to the hovels! The French Revolution accepted its European, its ecumenical role. It created the tricolor—red, white and blue—and the "Marseillaise."

Napoleon has been called the executor of the will of the French Revolution. This he was in so far as he maintained and defended its economical and legal achievements. In the *Code Napoléon* he laid down the legal basis of bourgeois rule. He brought about modernization and extension of education for the benefit of the middle classes. His armies carried his reforms deep into feudal and semi-feudal Europe. However, at the same time, he limited many of the hard-won political rights conquered during the revolutionary years. He directed the full power of united, centralized, middle class France to the conquest of an empire destined to exploit the world for the benefit of the French bourgeoisie and the Napoleonic armies. While the armies undermined medieval privileges and promoted mercantile and industrial activity, the regime became unpopular as a result of conscription, war levies and an economic policy exclusively geared to the interests of France and the ruin of its mighty competitor, Great Britain.

3.

Thus, in a new wave of nationalism, waxing especially high in Germany, the peoples rose against Napoleon, and his reign ended in 1815 at Waterloo. He left a changed continent with an alerted and strengthened bourgeoisie eager to learn from England the secrets of the Industrial Revolution. A young generation, inspired by 1791 and 1793, dreamt of liberal constitutions, republics and national liberation. To its sorrow, the armies that overthrew Napoleon were headed by the old autocratic rulers of Europe, the Tsar of Russia and in his wake the Emperor of Austria and the King of Prussia, backed by the British government of Whig and Tory aristocrats, which wanted neither a new and contagious 1793 nor a continental expansion of the Industrial Revolution. Thus for a period reaction was enforced under the banner of the so-called Holy Alliance.

The Holy Alliance of Christian Princes was formed in 1815, at the Tsar's invitation, by the sovereigns of Russia, Austria and Prussia. It was joined by almost all European monarchs. Its guiding spirit was the Austrian diplomat, Count von Metternich. At the Congress of Vienna, 1814–15, the map of Europe was redrawn for the benefit of the autocrats. Prussia obtained the Rhine province, economically the most advanced section of Germany. Germany remained a loose federation of states led by Prussia; Poland, carved up between Russia, Austria and Prussia since the partitions of 1772, 1793 and 1795, remained partitioned; Italy was divided between Austria, the Pope and two reactionary kings. France got its Bourbons back and with them a crowd of refugee nobles who had neither learned nor forgotten anything. Great Britain increased its already swollen empire, and joined Russia, Austria and Prussia in the Quadruple Alliance— an alliance of states, not of Christian princes, to which France, now safely Bourbon, was added in 1818. To all appearances the old regime had been restored, liberalism and revolution destroyed. Russia, Austria and Prussia would preserve the status quo, as a popular rhyme of the day expressed it:

> *Die irdische Trinität, Gott nachgeschaffen,*
> *So wie der Mensch sich widerholt im Affen.*
>
> *The Trinity on earth, God imitated,*
> *Just as man in monkey is recreated.*

The Holy Alliance lasted several decades, but in the long run could not withstand the underlying economic forces. Gradually capitalism penetrated deeply into the Europe of the Holy Alliance. In England the Industrial Revolution advanced at an ever increasing tempo. Machines, free competition, rapid accumulation, smoking factory towns, and an industrial bourgeoisie, depending for its wealth on a class of dispossessed wage workers, began to dominate British society, especially after the Napoleonic wars. All this could not be kept indefinitely from continental Europe.

A model of the new factory towns was Manchester, the cotton manufacturing center of England, situated near a coal mining district and connected with other sections of Great Britain by turnpikes and canals, and after 1825 by railroads. It was controlled by its factory owners, the new industrial middle class. The workers, men, women and children, recruited from ruined artisans, ruined farmers and poorhouses, many of them from Ireland, England's oldest colony, lived in jerry-built slums surrounding the mines and factories. Industry flourished not only on the growing home market, but on exports to all parts of the world; between 1780 and 1800 Manchester's exports of cotton goods increased 38-fold. No wonder that the impact of the Industrial Revolution affected the domestic economy of many countries. No wonder that the British manufacturers believed in free competition and free trade, and in the least possible interference by governments in their market transactions according to the well-known phrase: *laissez faire, laissez passer.*

Continental Europe, still overwhelmingly rural and agricultural, slowly began to cultivate its own factory system, its own modern capitalism. The growing bourgeoisie, centered mainly in France, Belgium and sections of Germany, felt more and more the archaic forms of government as shackles on the expansion of production. Thus the restored rule of autocracy came increasingly into contradiction with the reality of the new productive forces. The bourgeoisie became part of the opposition, and felt sympathy for the young nationalists and democrats—at any rate, so long as they did not rock the boat too much. In periods of crisis, as during the July revolution of 1830 in France, the bourgeoisie might even unfurl the tricolor and sing the "Marseillaise."

The first half of the 19th century is thus crowded with struggles against absolutism and *Gottesgnadentum,* monarchies by the grace of God. This opposition brought, at any rate until the revolutionary wave of 1830, a kind of uneasy alliance among all elements, moderate or radical, constitutionalist or republican, nationalist or internationalist, which in some way derived their ideas from *the* Revolution. For the sovereigns by the grace of God and Metternich all such ideas were equally repulsive and conjured up visions of *sans-culottes,* of Robespierre and the guil-

lotine. They answered the opposition by censorship, police sur-
veillance, imprisonment and even executions. The police were
everywhere. Secret agents, spies, *mouchards* and *Spitzel* infested
private and public life. Rebels thrown into prison have left moving stories of their sufferings; a classic is *My Prisons* (1831),
written by the Italian patriot, Silvio Pellico, who spent ten years
in Austrian prisons.[2] People were keenly police-conscious; the
detective story as a popular literary form dates from this period.

Struggles for national liberation were first in strongest evi-
dence outside the centers of capitalist development, in Ireland,
Italy, Poland and Latin America. These struggles meant action
for national consolidation as well. Police and army terror was
often answered by secret societies like the *Carbonari* (literally
charcoal burners) in Italy, which were surrounded by a halo of
romanticism. More open, but far more innocent, were the German *Burschenschaften* (fraternities) where students drank beer,
sang patriotic songs and even might shout: *Fürsten, zum Land
hinaus!*—out of the country, you princes! Even they were suppressed when in 1819 a student killed a Russian spy.[3] In Russia
we witness the short-lived rebellion of the Decembrists (1825), in
which Pushkin was involved. The only successful national struggles were those of the Greeks and the Latin Americans—breaks
in the status quo which were possible only because here the interests of the ruling powers collided. The Greek rebellion of
1822–29 will always be remembered because of the enthusiasm
it aroused among all liberals, radicals, romanticists and classi-
cists in Europe and America,[4] very much like the enthusiasm
felt by progressives for the Spanish Loyalists during 1936–39
and for the Vietnamese patriots at present.

4.

Up to 1830 the powers of reaction were able to keep the opposition under strict control despite occasional flare-ups. The
first major outbreak came in 1830, the July revolution in
France. It inspired revolutionary actions in Italy, Germany, the
Netherlands and Poland; in England a strong popular movement
forced passage of the Reform Act.

In France the reactionary Bourbon, Charles X, fled and was replaced by Louis Philippe of Orleans, the "bourgeois king," after three days of street fighting behind barricades, the so-called *Glorieuses*. But the working masses again pulled the chestnuts out of the fire for their betters. The wealthy bourgeoisie took over and soon exorcised the specter of 1793. Guizot, the historian who became a national leader, expressed the spirit of the new ruling class of bankers, wealthy industrialists and speculators with his slogan *Enrichissez vous!*—enrich yourselves! And enrich themselves they did, these new rulers, building industries, factories, mines and railroads, and letting capitalism get hold of France in an orgy of speculation. The bitterly disappointed radical democrats had to fall back to their clubs and their presses. The new constitution had abolished censorship, and newspapers of all political shades could now appear. The government knew no respite from the ceaseless barrage of opposition which even led to insurrection, as in 1832, 1834 and 1839. Cartoonists had a heyday; the world still enjoys the biting sketches of Daumier and Gavarni. In this wave of opposition literature flourished; Balzac and Stendhal, in some of their greatest novels, mercilessly dissected the new bourgeois society. Paris, already the hub of European science, also became the hub of European radicalism.

England escaped the barricades, but it passed through a severe political crisis under the pressure of mass meetings and strikes. This crisis led to the passage of the Reform Act of 1832, which did for Great Britain what the July Revolution had done for France. Again the working masses were bypassed. The ancient Tory and Whig aristocracy had to share far more of its political power with the wealthy industrial and commercial middle class, but, as in France, the electoral franchise was extended without reaching the working class. The Whig historian Macaulay could proclaim in parliament that universal suffrage was utterly incompatible with the very existence of civilization.

Industrially advanced Belgium made itself independent from the Northern Netherlands. The political systems of Great Britain, France and Belgium were now fundamentally the same: in power were moderate liberals representing the wealthier sections of the bourgeoisie under a constitutional monarch. They were somewhat in the stage envisioned by the French Constitution of 1791. They enjoyed considerable freedom of the press and of assembly. But those in power were loath to consider any further political reforms: no 1793 for them. If before 1830 there was a half-hearted coalition between moderate liberals and radical democrats, it now ceased to exist. The United States (aside from Switzerland) was still the only republic, but also here an active democratic movement set in, that of the "militant thirties."

Outside of these countries the revolutionary movement met with total failure. Austria continued to rule Italy, the German princes continued to rule their own subjects. The Poles rebelled against the Tsar in a heroic uprising, which was greeted by the liberal and radical elements of Europe and America with an enthusiasm comparable to that felt for the Greeks only a few years before. But all this enthusiasm was of no avail; in 1831 the Poles were crushed by Russian armies. Exiled Poles kept the flame burning in the capitals of Western Europe.

This was the period in which Giuseppe Mazzini (1805–72) began his patriotic propaganda, democratic, vaguely socialistic, with conspiratorial and messianic overtones. In 1830 he joined the Carbonari. Soon exiled from Italy, he formed abroad leagues of young patriots, his Young Italy, soon followed by Young Poland, Young France, Young Switzerland, Young Europe. In Germany this type of romantic patriotic enthusiasm was paralleled by Young Germany. Many members of these societies were emigrants or exiles; Paris, Zürich, Geneva and London had large colonies of immigrants, mostly artisans, but also students, representing a broad spectrum of political thought. The Germans were known for their beer parlors and glee clubs (Sangvereine).

Despite widespread discontent, reaction continued until it reached its height around 1840. Then the economic necessities began to prevail increasingly over the political restraints. The new middle classes began to demand greater political influence, pressed from the left by radical artisans and intellectuals. They had to fight tooth and nail; autocracy refused to give in one inch more than it had to. Yet it was willing to grant concessions if its own interests could also be served. In 1834 almost all German states (but not Austria) united in a general customs union, the *Zollverein*, which greatly stimulated industrial and mercantile expansion. In 1835 the first railroad was opened in Germany. But, without the tradition and the cumulative experience of the British and French, the German bourgeoisie remained politically weak and submissive. The great national problems remained unsolved while the economic conditions were changing rapidly. Bourgeois, workers and students were increasingly discontented. A new revolution could be anticipated at the first sign of a political or economic crisis, and again it would be heralded by the crowing of the Gallic rooster. The crisis set in during 1847.

5.

Not only had the bourgeoisie grown in number and strength, but so also had the proletariat. This fact was demonstrated in all clarity in Great Britain, the oldest and most mature capitalist country. In the beginning of the Industrial Revolution wage workers, in despair, rebelled wildly, even smashing machines, as during the Luddite revolts of 1811–12. But gradually a new and revolutionary change took shape: the wage workers began to organize themselves as an independent class, with its own forms of struggle, its own budding consciousness, demands, policies, and organizations. Trade unions were launched. At first they were severely prosecuted under the existing anti-combination laws, but this was countered by mounting resistance, shown in strikes and mass demonstrations. A deep impression was made when in 1819 a meeting of 60,000 workers in Manchester was savagely attacked by the militia; the brutal event became known as the massacre of Peterloo. It inspired Shelley to write his "Mask of Anarchy":

> *Rise, like lions after slumber,*
> *In unvanquishable number,*
> *Shake your chains to earth like dew*
> *Which in sleep has fallen on you.*
> *Ye are many, they are few!*

Workers, humanitarians, and even the landed aristocrats were horrified. Pressure for legislation against the fierce exploitation in factories and mines was strong enough to lead in 1819 to the first law against child labor, prohibiting the labor of children under—nine years! Older children were not to be employed above —72 hours a week! In 1825 the right to organize trade unions, including the right to strike, was recognized by law.

Trade unionism now began to flourish; federations of trade unions followed—a transition from trade-union to trades-union.[5] Persecution never stopped; the British working class still remembers the "Tolpuddle martyrs"—agricultural laborers who tried to organize, were arrested in 1834 and given seven years deportation, a severe sentence, but one that aroused great opposition.

Agitation continued in a new, more massive form after the disappointing Reform Act of 1832. In 1838 a People's Charter* was drawn up to formulate the political demands of the militant workers; it stood for universal suffrage for men, secret ballot and other electoral reforms. The Charter was endorsed in thousands of meetings; a petition to Parliament received 1,280,000 signatures. As Parliament refused to act, the workers became more rebellious; the men of property rallied and banded together against a massive but poorly led working class. By 1840 most Chartist leaders were in jail, the movement seemed broken.

But the Chartist movement revived stronger than ever, under the bitter necessity of an economic depression. Its revival coincided in time with the strengthening of the whole radical movement on the Continent, so that the democratic movements of the whole of Europe began to come closer together. In 1842 the Chartists drew up a new petition which received as many as 3,500,000 signatures. At one time the Chartist League counted 40,000 members. Chartism seemed to reach a climax early in 1847, and was followed by the February Revolution in France. A new petition to Parliament was presented, which was to be accompanied by a mass demonstration in London in April 1848.

* So called after the "Magna Charta" of 1215.

The climax, however, turned into an anticlimax because of poor leadership unable to face a united propertied class. The demonstration was a failure, the petition scornfully rejected.

Chartism might have again recovered from this blow but for the failure of the continental revolution, aggravating dissension among the leaders, and the upswing of the economy after 1848. These and other factors contributed to the downward trend in the radical movement of the forties. However, the labor movement was not destroyed, as on the Continent; it turned more and more to "pure" trade unionism, now that capitalism had shown its capacity for strong revival. In this way Chartist demands were pressed upon a bourgeoisie gradually getting adjusted to the existence of a labor movement, and most of these demands were eventually introduced into law, as in the Second Reform Act of 1867. What also remained was the inspiring example of the first mass working class movement in history.

It was in the nature of capitalist development that the labor movement started later on the Continent than in Britain. The French labor movement may be said to have started with the revolt of Lyons silk weavers, the *canuts,* coming out of their horrid sweatshops onto the streets in 1831, and then again in 1834, addressing their bosses:

> *When our reign arrives*
> *When your reign shall end*
> *Then we shall weave the shroud of the old world*
> *For hear! revolt is rumbling*—[6]

Insurrections in other cities followed, all cruelly suppressed. The massacre of the Paris Rue Transnonain is still remembered, if only through the savage cartoon of Daumier. A result of the suppression of labor's activity was the beginning of socialist influence in the ranks of artisans and proletarians. Socialism, so far a bourgeois and petty-bourgeois movement, began to penetrate the mines, the wharves, the work- and sweatshops. Since the socialists were also increasingly active in the Chartist movement, we can date the early beginnings of labor's approach to socialism, and socialism's approach to labor, from this period.

Germany came after France. Here we witness the beginnings of independent working class action in the revolt of the Silesian weavers in 1844. This revolt, in its bitter fight against inhuman sweatshop conditions, as well as in its cruel suppression, has much in common with the events of 1834 in Lyons. Again, it left an indelible impression upon the labor movement and far beyond. The German movement still remembers the song of the weavers:

> *In this place there is a court*
> *Much worse than all the Fehmen**
> *Where no one needs a court and judge*
> *To quickly kill a person.*[7]

It also remembers the poem by Heinrich Heine:

> *Without a tear in their grim eyes,*
> *They sit at the loom, the rage of despair on their faces:*
> *We have suffered and hunger'd long enough;*
> *Old Germany, we are weaving a shroud for thee*
> *And weaving it with a triple curse.*
> *We are weaving, weaving.*[8]

This revolt is also the topic of Gerhard Hauptmann's stirring play *Die Weber* (The Weavers, 1892).

The time had come also on the Continent of Europe when the working class was beginning to emerge as an independent force, no longer voiceless or tied to the ruling class. Its own demands could now be heard. The Revolution of 1848 forced the capitalist world to take notice of this new independent force that was ready to challenge the ancient order.

* *Fehmen:* medieval kangaroo courts.

II. THE INTELLECTUAL FERMENT

Laws and rights move through the ages
Like an unending slow disgrace.
They hobble through the generations,
And softly steal from place to place.
What clever was grows into nonsense
And benefice becomes a plight.
Unlucky grandson, you be pitied,
Nobody offers you your right.

—Goethe, *Faust*, 1808[1]

If sympathy proclaims that the exploitation of man by man must disappear completely; if it is true that mankind is moving toward a state of things in which all men, without distinction of birth, will receive from society according to their merits and be remunerated according to their work; then it is evident that the constitution of property must be changed. . . .

—Bazard and Enfantin, 1829[2]

1.

The year 1845 marks the beginning of Marxism as a new world outlook, a materialist philosophy with its own approach to the problems of the labor movement. To understand it we must have a look at the spiritual and social setting in which it originated.

What strikes us in this period is its intellectual ferment. The ferment extended into all fields: science, literature, arts, philosophy, religion, even reaching into such domains as music and mathematics. Beethoven's *Ninth Symphony*, with Schiller's *Alle Menschen werden Brüder* (all men will be brothers), Goethe's *Faust II*, Heine's, Shelley's and Keats' poems, Dickens' and Balzac's novels belong to this period. A feeling of heroism, of epic

25

grandeur, runs through the best of literature. Faust and Prometheus, the legendary fighters for man's delivery from the powers of darkness, are invoked: "Prometheus," wrote Marx in his doctor's dissertation, "is the principal saint in the philosophical calendar." Writers, poets, philosophers were openly partisan, for or against the spirit of the French Revolution, some looking forward with expectation, others backward with nostalgia. It was the period of romanticism, and romanticism was history-conscious.

Europe had become vividly aware of the great changes that had occurred and were constantly occurring in all domains of life as a result of the Revolution. It filled many with hope: "It was a splendid sunshine," wrote Hegel in his *Philosophy of History;* "all thinking human beings have participated in celebrating this epoch." The search for the *meaning* of history pervaded literary and academic circles; leading historians tried not only to chronicle but to *interpret* what had been and what was happening. The British and the French revolutions became the subject of intensive research, each author having his own axe to grind. Marx would learn much from the historians Thierry and Guizot, who came close to an interpretation of the French and English revolutions as a struggle of social classes; Thierry had been secretary to Saint-Simon, the great utopian reformer and interpreter of society in evolution, seen as a result of property relationships. This was indeed a far cry from the static philosophy of the Enlightenment with its stress on eternal and immutable laws like those of Newton. Law, philosophy, theology, religion, art were seen in their historical perspective; revolutionary breaks occurred in many fields. To cite only a few examples, we think of the bible critique of Strauss, the new linguistics of the Grimms, the new mathematical physics, the new geometries, the discovery of the cell, as well as the critique of society culminating in socialism and communism. With the deepening of the sense of history came the concept of evolution, gradual or sudden, and the question not only of the meaning, but of the *direction* of history. Can we look not only into the past but also into the future, and thus make sense of history? Hegel went deep into all these questions in terms of his dialectics. Soon, in Marx's hands, these different strains converged into a new philosophical outlook, dialectical and historical materialism.

2.

This is the period of the rise of socialism. The disillusion following the defeat of the Jacobins, the Napoleonic and post-Napoleonic reaction, the abandonment by the bourgeoisie of the ideals of liberty, equality and fraternity, the widespread misery in the wake of advancing technology, left many socially aware persons deeply disturbed. The economists, following Adam Smith and David Ricardo, had proclaimed that capitalism was the natural order of things. It was necessary to show that this "natural order" was in reality unnatural, that it could be broken, that there were social structures possible far more in conformity with human nature and far less dismal.

The men who took this approach became known as socialists and communists, depending on the degree of their radicalism.[3] An early representative in England was William Godwin (1756–1836), author of *Inquiry Concerning Political Justice* (1793) with a plea for a system of full equality in a society without state pressure. Godwin is therefore often considered the "father" of anarchism, that brand of radicalism which considers all state power as evil. Another early fighter for an egalitarian form of social justice was Gracchus Babeuf (1760–97) in France, the leader of the Conspiracy of the Equals under the Directory. He called for the reintroduction and strengthening of the Constitution of 1793 so that social and economic equality could be reached in a society without private property. His organization prepared for an armed uprising, but was betrayed by a spy. Its leaders were executed or exiled.[4]

When, in the heady political atmosphere after the Revolution of 1830, socialist doctrines received a new lease on life, the ideas of the Equals found an influential spokesman in Philippe Bounarotti (1761–1837), an ancient Babouvist, exiled and at last, in 1830, back in France. In 1828 he had published the history of the Babouvist conspiracy in his *Conspiration pour l'égalité dite de Babeuf,* establishing an historic link between the radicals of 1789 and of 1830. Thus Marx became acquainted with the Babouvist ideas and although he saw the Equals as "crude, uncivilized materialists," he appreciated them as vigorous champions of the workers, giving the first example of a communist party and *carriers of a new world order.*[5]

By the time Buonarotti's agitation reached France, the schemes of two radical reformers were being widely discussed. They were Claude Henri, Count of Saint-Simon (1760–1825; he renounced the title at the time of the Revolution) and Charles Fourier (1772–1837). They are, with their English contemporary Robert Owen (1771–1850), known as the great utopians; Engels, in his *Socialism, Utopian and Scientific,* has given a masterful sketch of these leading reformers of their age. It is sufficient to recall that both Saint-Simon and Fourier developed schemes of the good society as they envisioned it, Saint-Simon more in general outlines, Fourier in precise details.

Both were keen critics of the bourgeois social order, both had a sense of history, especially Saint-Simon. Neither of them had an understanding of the revolutionary role of the proletariat. Saint-Simon saw in history a struggle of classes, but for him they were the unproductive class of landlords, priests and rentiers, and the productive class of men engaged in science and industry, employers, technicians and wage workers. His ideal society was to be governed by a global "economic parliament" of artists, scientists and industrialists, with bankers as executives.[6] Fourier's ideal society consisted of workers living in inner and outer harmony in beautiful community houses called *phalanstères,* and he always hoped for wealthy patrons willing to donate the funds to start his socialist communities. These patrons never turned up, but *phalanstères* have been tried, especially in the United States.[7] They were all of short duration.

Neither the pupils of Saint-Simon nor of Fourier were interested in political activity; they relied on persuasion of well-meaning men and women. The Saint-Simonians, under the leadership of Bazard and Enfantin, were for a while very popular, especially between 1825 and 1832, among scientists and engineers with a social conscience. Their teachings were summarized in aphorisms such as:

All social institutions should aim at the moral, intellectual and physical improvement of the most numerous and poorest class.
All privileges of birth to be abolished without exception.
The task of each be according to his capacity, the wealth of each be according to his works.[8]

The more ardent Saint-Simonians soon started a rather absurd religious cult under "Father" Enfantin as the bearded Messiah. The others dispersed; many capitulated to the charms of the Second Empire of Napoleon III, becoming leading administrators and engineers. One of them, De Lesseps, became the moving spirit in the construction of the Suez Canal. Others followed less glorious paths: "Under the Second Empire," wrote Mehring in his *History of German Social-Democracy*, "the crudest forms of fraud on the stock market took place under the banner of Saint-Simonism," and the poet Heine mocked that the only cross the former martyrs carried was the cross of the Legion of Honor.

The Fourierists remained very active under the leadership of Victor Considérant (1808–93). Of his voluminous writings we only mention his confession of faith, the *Principes du socialisme, manifeste de la démocratie au dix-neuvième siècle* (1843) — Principles of Socialism, Manifesto of Democracy in the Nineteenth Century—since it has often been cited as the source of inspiration for the *Communist Manifesto*—incorrectly, as we shall see.

Christian socialism was represented by the eloquent prophet Félicité de Lamennais (1782–1854). His *Paroles d'un croyant* (1833) —Words of a Believer— was a passionate plea for social justice. Translated into many languages and passing through more than a hundred editions, it was so influential that the Pope issued a special bull condemning it as *libellum, mole quidam exiguum pravitate tamen ingentium*—a book small in size but huge in its depravity. But Lamennais continued to plead for his ideal Christian community, meanwhile sharply criticizing the Saint-Simonians and other socialist sects as willing to sacrifice the freedom of the individual to the collective. Lamennais tried to accomplish inside the Catholic world that which somewhat later was undertaken in England among the Protestants by the influential divines, F. D. Maurice and Charles Kingsley. It seems that the latter coined the term "Christian socialist." Incidentally, it was the clergyman Kingsley who, independently of Marx, discovered that religion is the "opium of the people."*

These utopian writers saw class conflicts primarily as moral conflicts. They did not address the working people, seeing in them only the poor and disinherited, not the potentially revolutionary fighters. Being in the first place radical philanthropists, utopians, they spoke by preference to the enlightened bourgeoisie.

However, with the increase in size and importance of the working classes, whether poor artisans or factory hands, a new generation of socialists appeared which expressed in varying degrees the aspirations of these sections of the population, although with still a good deal of utopianism. We may call them the doctrinaire socialists, and among them we find Louis Blanc, Etienne Cabet and Pierre Joseph Proudhon. All of them believed in peaceful transition. Of these, Proudhon was by far the most talented thinker.

Proudhon (1809–1865) was the first leading French socialist with a proletarian background. He was one of those roving artisans traveling from place to place to eke out a living—*ein wandernder Geselle,* as they say in German—who play such a vital role in this stage of development and spread of socialist thought. He was a printer, self-educated, and first gained fame with his eloquent and provocative book *Qu'est-ce-que la propriété?* (1840) —What is Property? His answer was: Property is theft. This is typical of Proudhon, whose extensive body of writings is full of such contradictions. Stripped of them, his main theme is that man should live in free association in a kind of federalist organization of social and national groupings. The ideal was anarchy; Proudhon coined the term in its modern sense. But his

* "We have used the Bible as . . . an opium dose for keeping beasts of burden patient while they were being overloaded" (1848) .

radicalism could not hide the fact that Proudhon's doctrine amounted to an appeal for such reforms as would substantially benefit small producers and proprietors, and not the factory worker. Marx later called Proudhon *petit-bourgeois.* In accordance with his theory, Proudhon rejected the seizure of political power. However, for several generations his philosophy had a strong appeal to workers in France, Italy and Spain with little or no experience of modern industry, hence to small town and agricultural workers, whose militancy tended toward anarchism and syndicalism. In contrast, Marx's philosophy appealed to the experience of the modern proletariat, to which Proudhon always showed an aversion.[9]

The militants were usually organized in secret societies with fancy names such as Society of the Families or Society of the Seasons. They were engaged not only in communist propaganda, but also in plotting the violent seizure of the government. They were behind the insurrections of 1832, 1834, and 1839; in the latter the Paris city hall was even for a short time held by the rebels. The leaders were Auguste Blanqui (1805–1884) and Armand Barbès (1809–1870), both outstanding representatives of the professional revolutionary activist, a type that now begins to appear. Tireless conspirators, selfless devotees to the cause as they saw it, they had to spend many years in prison. Blanqui saw communism as the result of a historical development resulting from the actions of a more and more enlightened public, until at last "the triumvirate of Loyola, Caesar, and Shylock" would be overcome. Marx had great respect for Blanqui, his dedication and adherence to the ideal of communism. But Marx saw the historical road to communism in the political and economic organization of the working class and not, like Blanqui, in the conspiratorial activity of a group of dedicated agitators plotting a *coup d'état* without taking into account all the basic factors that make a revolutionary situation.[10]

3.

The Chartist movement in Great Britain was a loose united front formed by the most varied elements: pure trade unionists, fighters for the ten-hour day, friends of cooperatives, radical democrats, bourgeois reformers, humanitarians, advocates of moral persuasion and advocates of violence. There were also socialists among them. Their senior was Robert Owen.

Owen knew the modern factory system from the inside, since he had been the director of a large and profitable cotton mill in Scotland, where he had introduced working conditions which for the time were exemplary. Yet he felt more and more that the whole wage system was bad; his workers stayed in bondage. He agitated for the establishment of experimental cooperative communities, and from 1825 to 1828 conducted with his son such a community on a socialist basis at New Harmony in present Indiana.

After its failure he turned more and more to the labor unions as a sounding board for his theories and was active in the cooperative and Chartist movements. It was in his weekly, *The New Moral World,* that Engels wrote some of his first English articles (1843–1845). But Owen never understood that the class struggle itself develops the forces necessary for the overthrow of capitalism; he always clung to his belief in moral persuasion through the examples of model settlements, cooperatives, and labor banks. Thus he remained, like Saint-Simon and Fourier, a utopian. But he was one of the first socialists to bring his message to the labor movement where it belongs.

The silver-tongued orator of the Chartist movement, Feargus O'Connor (1796–1855), was hardly a socialist, although he dabbled in cooperative associations. In 1837 he began to edit *The Northern Star,* which became the leading Chartist paper. Two of its editors, Ernest Jones (1819–60) and George Julian Harney (1817–97), were militant trade unionists. Young Engels, then a clerk in a Manchester textile firm, contacted Harney and became a contributor.[11] Both Jones and Harney were to become sympathetic to the ideas of Marx and Engels; Harney became a life-long friend. Perhaps the keenest political mind of the movement was James Bronterre O'Brien (1802–64), "the Chartist schoolmaster." A pupil of Owen, he had communist sympathies; in 1836 he published an English verison of Buonarotti's

history of Babeuf's conspiracy. This shows that the socialist ideas began to stretch across the sea; he, Jones and Harney belonged to those left-wing Chartists who began to see the movement in international terms. Harney was an organizer of a "Feast of Nations" held in London in September 1845, a banquet to commemorate the establishment of the French Republic in 1792. More than a thousand enthusiasts from many nations participated and cheered. Harney was one of the speakers. Shortly afterward he was among the organizers of the Society of Fraternal Democrats uniting the revolutionary exiles from the continent with the radical wing of the Chartists. In November 1847 this society organized another international meeting in London, commemorating the anniversary of the Polish insurrection of 1830. Among the speakers were Harney, Jones, Marx and Engels.[12]

4.

Socialism came to Germany only in the late 1830's, although writings by and about Saint-Simon and Fourier were already known in certain intellectual circles. Its apostle was a tailor named Wilhelm Weitling (1808–71). Like Proudhon he was born and bred in poverty; like him he led the life of a roving artisan. Reading voraciously after long working hours he gave himself an education and became a leader of radical workers, first in Germany, then in Switzerland and France. He organized workers' societies as recruiting grounds for socialist clubs, often secret or semi-secret. His teaching was communist, actively revolutionary, inspired by the Bible.

We find him in 1835 in Paris, where there were hundreds of German artisans, mainly tailors and carpenters, and here he associated with the left-wing League of the Proscribed (Bund der Geächteten). After a stay in Switzerland he was back in Paris during 1837–41; there he agitated as a leading spirit of the League of the Just (Bund der Gerechten), organized in 1836 after a split in the radical wing of the Proscribed. The League was connected with Blanqui's Seasons and had members elsewhere, even in Germany. In 1838 his confession of faith ap-

peared: *Die Menschheit wie sie ist und wie sie sein sollte*—Humanity, as It Is and as It Should Be—influenced by Lamennais, and published at great sacrifice with the hard-earned pennies of his many devoted followers. In 1841 he went to Switzerland to assist in the organization of branches of the Just. Here he wrote his main work, *Die Garantien der Harmonie und der Freiheit* (1842) —Guarantees of Harmony and Freedom, followed by the more popular, *Das Evangelism eines armen Sünders* (1845) —the Gospel of a Poor Sinner. Here he proclaimed in prophetic language, like a revivalist preacher, his gospel of revolution, liberation and equality, attacked the forces of money and property, and called for a Messiah to lead the workers to a society of equals governed by scientists and sages. The workers, said Weitling, have no fatherland, which is a misconception foisted upon them by property owners. Jesus was a communist, primitive Christianity a shining example of equality and brotherhood.[13]

These books served, in the forties, as a kind of Communist bible for the German-speaking revolutionary workers. Marx, in his early days as a communist, thought highly of them. Where, he asked, could the bourgeoisie show such a work as Weitling's *Guarantees* in regard to its own emancipation? And he added: "It must be said that the German proletariat is the theoretician of the European proletariat just as the English proletariat is its political economist and the French its politician."[14]

A few years later Marx was far more critical of Weitling, and resented in particular his messianic eqalitarianism, which led to mere phraseology and empty generalities. In 1846 it came to a break. Weitling, who after imprisonment in Switzerland had been wandering through Germany, England and Belgium, emigrated to the United States. Here, for many years, he was an active organizer of German immigrant artisans, but also indulged in chimerical utopian schemes. He never understood the necessity of political struggle, not even at the time of the Civil War.[15] In contrast to him, the Marxian immigrant Joseph Weydemeyer (1818–68) became an abolitionist and later saw active service as a colonel in the Civil War.[16]

5.

Other, non-socialist, strands were woven into the fabric of the philosophy of Marx and Engels. Where most socialists merely indicted capitalist society, these two felt the need to understand the mechanism. Where most socialists only stressed the desirability of a new world order, Marx and Engels sought the dynamics by which the change could be performed. This required a new outlook on the whole social and intellectual order, and for this they found the *method* in the highest form of philosophical thinking then developed, in German classical philosophy, and in particular in Hegel's dialectics. In British classical economy they recognized the first attempt at a serious scientific analysis of the economics of capitalist society.

Great Britain had had its bourgeois revolution as early as the 17th century. Although it did not destroy the big landed estates it gave the middle classes considerable freedom to operate. During the 18th century capitalist industry was so well advanced that in 1776 the Scot Adam Smith could formulate the laws of this capitalist, free enterprise system with impressive clarity. In his *Inquiry into the Nature and Causes of the Wealth of Nations* he reduced politics, social activity and public morality to economic categories and recognized property as the essence of the structure of society. The greatest hope for the increase of the wealth of nations lay in the activity of sovereign individuals pursuing their natural self-interest, as far as possible unchecked. This increase was made possible by the improvements in the productive powers of labor, due to the division of labor. The "three great, original and constituent orders of every civilized society" were "the orders of people who live by rent, who live by wages and who live by profit." Their reward was based on the most equal of all relationships, the exchange of commodities on a free and open market. Removal of the obstacles to this open market meant the pursuit of wealth and progress. Thus the two fundamental ideas of Smith were self-interest and natural liberty.

Smith was aware that labor* measures the value of a commodity, and that the interests of employers and workers were in
conflict. Yet he claimed that both parties received an advantage
from increase in natural wealth. This claim, however, was soon
placed in serious doubt by the further development of the factory system. Humanitarians and radicals objected, refusing to
believe that Smith's "natural" order was so natural after all.
Godwin preached his ideal community based on equality of all
and was attacked by the pastor Thomas Malthus, in his *Essay on
the Principles of Population* (1798). Here Malthus tried to
prove mathematically that inequality, and hence poverty, is in
the very nature of things because population tends to grow much
faster than the means of subsistence. When David Ricardo in his
Principles of Political Economy (1819) reformulated Smith's
theory in a more rigorous form, it was against Malthus' and Ricardo's "natural" order that the arrows of humanitarian and radical, as well as conservative, critiques were mainly aimed. Political economy became known as the "dismal" science.

These theories, amounting to a scientific analysis of the new,
the capitalist society, were ignored by almost all socialists who
relied more on appeals to humanitarian principles. One of the
great steps forward taken by Marx and Engels was their realization that socialists should *understand* the laws underlying capitalist society because the operation of these laws leads to the
possibility of socialism. What *is* and what *should be*, in direct
contradiction to the utopians, stand in dialectical unity for Marx
and Engels. Their study revealed serious weaknesses in the classical theories of Smith and Ricardo. Marx's analysis, which was
to culminate in his discovery of the theory of surplus value,
showed that the "natural" order of the classical economists was
not natural but transitory. In the creation of a proletariat the
capitalist order contained the elements of its own destruction and
its replacement by a socialist order. The "dismal theory" was
turned into one of the pillars of a new theoretical edifice, that of
liberation of the working class. Marx and Engels had already
started out on this work years before the writing of the *Manifes-*

* Marx would later correct this to "labor power."

to—around 1844 when Engels was in Manchester, Marx in Paris. The final results were laid down, after more than 20 years of work, in the first volume of *Capital* (1867), to be followed later by two other volumes.

In Germany, as we have seen, the middle class was weak, propaganda for radical political change discouraged or *verboten*. Yet the intellectual heritage was strong and deeply affected by the events of 1789. The existing ferment found an outlet in the world of ideas. Great battles were fought in academic halls, books, periodicals and beer parlors. It was the great creative period in philosophy, the time of the quartet—Kant, Fichte, Schelling, Hegel. These thinkers translated the political and social longings of Germany's intellectuals into the search for the laws and hence for the freedom of the mind. Our main attention must go to Hegel, at the climax of German classical philosophy.

Where the 17th-century philosophers Descartes and Leibniz searched for a universal science capable of solving all problems of nature, Hegel searched for a universal method capable of approaching the whole of the mind's empire. His *Phaenomenologie des Geistes* (1806) —Phenomenology of the Mind—is a veritable journey on the three levels of personal, historical and ontological experience through all stages of human endeavor and thought until finally the mind in contemplation of the World Spirit finds true understanding and its final freedom.

Hegel's method consisted in giving a novel and dynamic content to the ancient Greek concept of oral dispute, called dialectics. In Hegel's teachings all concepts are placed in their endless array of mutual relationships, each concept analyzed in its limitations and contradictions, so that it could be "negated" and "transcended" into a fuller, more embracing concept, and a new understanding reached concerning the previous concept. In his philosophy of law (which for Hegel was more than law or *Recht,* as he called it, but the whole social structure) he starts with abstract free will, from there goes to the person and his property, then to morality and to ethics. In developing these concepts he reaches from the family to civic society and from there to the conceptual climax, the State, as the "reality of the ethical idea." In relations among different states world history reveals itself:

Die Weltgeschichte ist das Weltgericht, world history is world judgment.

Concepts thus found their unity in their very contradictions, or, in Hegel's language, in the unity (also, identity) of opposites. Key concepts are consciousness, self-consciousness, alienation, potentiality and actuality, thus expressing development, evolution—but far more, since they lead to the identity of object and subject in the Absolute, the World Spirit.

This meant on the historical level that Hegel strove to find a *sense* in history, seeing it as the gradual evolution of the World Spirit. Where Smith, whom Hegel had read, searched for a permanent natural order and found it in the capitalism of his day, Hegel taught that everything in existence carries the elements of its own destruction—or better, transcendence—forming a link in a chain—a chain, as he saw it, of progress. World history was judgment, yes, but also the development of the concept of freedom. "It is the true theodicy, the justification of God in history."

This was idealism, not subjective but objective idealism, the subordination of the material world under the spell of the mind, seen as the World Spirit, the *Weltgeist.* But in terms of the social-economic world of Hegel's day, where did it lead? With all his appreciation of the French Revolution (even of Napoleon: the *Weltgeist* on horseback!) and the potentially revolutionary character of the dialectics, Hegel turned more and more conservative in his later days. Prussia, Germany, "got" him, as it "got" so many other brilliant men. His social theodicy ended with the Prussian State of his day, hopefully, but not necessarily, with a constitutional monarchy. He died in 1832, objecting to the July Revolution and the agitation for the Reform Bill in England.[17]

When we now try to read Hegel it is hard to believe that his highly technical jargon (interspersed with brilliant aphorisms) once set the spirit of an entire generation on fire. But "Hegelizing" was the fashion and it even spilled across the border: Proudhon's way of thinking is an example. This generation was passionately looking for a sense in history and found it in terms of Hegel's dialectics, every person in his own way. Many of the master's pupils, in the political atmosphere of the July Revolution and its aftermath, moved forward, turning more radical—first in religious matters (which, in Germany, was also a matter concerning the state), then also directly in the political arena. Hegel had looked into the past and present, they wanted to look into the future. Since they were used to expressing their ideas in the customary jargon of the self-development of the mind, these Young Hegelians to a certain extent could get away with it under the existing censorship and police supervision. When they began to be more explicit they naturally met all kinds of harassment.

The Young Hegelians were a companionable lot, at any rate in the years around 1840, when they and their cronies gathered in beer and wine halls to drink, sing, talk and discuss the papers and books they were writing or planning. Leading these *Berliner Freien* (Berlin Free) was the radical theologian Bruno Bauer (1809–82). He and his brother Edgar proclaimed the history of mankind as the development, not of Hegel's Absolute but of human "self-consciousness." The task of the philosopher was to direct self-consciousness into higher phases, to the full emancipation of the individual. This task they called the Critique. Remaining entirely in the realm of thought, undisturbed by the grit of everyday life, they sought their own emancipation from the "masses." Marx and Engels later ridiculed their snooty Critique as the "Critical Critique." Another leader was the publicist Arnold Ruge (1802–80); he had served six years in prison as a member of the *Burschenschaft* and thought in terms of radical political reform, a philosophy of action.* In the work of these leaders we see the beginning of the understanding that it is not the state that determines society, as in Hegel, but that society determines the State—a step, but only a first step, toward historical materialism. Marx and Engels frequented the *Freien* for some time, Marx when a student at Berlin University, Engels, a few months after Marx, while serving in the military. Both at that time looked to the Bauers and Ruge for leadership.

---

* This stress on a philosophy of action, *eine Philosophie der Tat,* was inspired by the memory of Fichte, who had been a passionate patriotic leader at the time of Prussia's humiliation by Napoleon.

The radical Young Hegelians were struggling in this way to pass from the nebulous domain of the spirit, where their master had stranded them, to the world of everyday life with its political problems. And so they felt the strong impact of another Hegelian, Ludwig Feuerbach (1804–72), when he argued for a complete reversal of Hegel's idealism, first in the field of religion, then in general philosophical speculation, in his *Wesen des Christenthums* (1841) —Essence of Christianity—and in his *Vorläufige Thesen zur Reformation der Philosophie* (1842) — Preliminary Theses toward the Reform of Philosophy.

Feuerbach returned, in a sense, to the materialism of the French Enlightenment, analyzing man as a product of nature, creating his ideas from his own life, or better, from the life of his whole *species,* in the struggle with nature around him. This sounds pretty obvious to most of us, but it came as a great eye-opener to those who for years had been operating with a disembodied Spirit. Moreover, Feuerbach enriched his materialism with some of Hegel's dialectical thinking. This led him to abandon the 18th century theory that religion is the product of priestly deceit and Hegel's conception of religion as a stage in the development of the World Spirit, and to look at religion as a product of man's alienation from nature and himself. In short, it is not God who creates man, but man who creates God. Thus Feuerbach placed man back in his natural environment, and tried to show that man can reach a humanist attitude toward his fellow man.

At this point, however, as Marx and Engels would show, he failed to advance far enough. He underestimated seriously the fact that man is also the product of his social environment with its conflicts. Feuerbach's man was still an abstraction from man as he really lives and acts. And secondly, another flaw in his dialectics, his philosophy was purely interpretative and lacked the dynamics necessary to inspire man to social, revolutionary action. No wonder that with all his sympathy for socialism in his moral philosophy he never moved much beyond the preaching of a general love of humanity. He stayed aloof from the class struggle.

Feuerbach thus remained wrapped up in his philosophical abstractions about man, or in his phrase, "species man," *Gattungsmensch,* collective man, in an attitude of remoteness from social struggles, strengthened by his solitary living in a small Franconian village. But for a while he inspired the most politically active among the Young Hegelians. "Enthusiasm was general; we all became at once Feuerbachians," wrote Engels many years later in retrospect.[18] By this time some Young Hegelians were turning away from mere political reform toward socialism, guided by Feuerbach's insistence that it was in the real world of collective man and his activity that the road to freedom lay. Marx was led toward socialism by his experiences as collaborator, later editor, of the democratic *Rheinische Zeitung* (1842–43), Engels by his experiences in the English textile industry and the Chartist movement (1843–45).

Still another young Hegelian who became a socialist via Feuerbach and a passion for the philosophy of action, even before Marx and Engels, was Moses Hess (1812–75). Hess was a Rhinelander like Marx and Engels. Beginning around 1837 he attempted to give a socialist color to the Jewish religion; the New Jerusalem, he claimed, could only be realized in a society without private property. During a stay in France he absorbed French socialism, which he studied, and enriched by his knowledge of Hegel and Feuerbach and of political economy; he came close to scientific socialism. But he never was able to think these ideas through with the dialectical consistency typical of Marx and Engels. Although during the years 1844–48 he often worked closely with these younger men, and his writings were advanced for his time, he became more and more alienated. There always remained a mystical religious element in Hess' thinking; in later years be became a forerunner of Zionism, although he always stayed faithful to the socialist labor movement.[19]

The vagueness in his thinking was shared by many German intellectuals who, in the years between 1844 and 1848, turned to socialism under the influence of German philosophy and some French-English socialism.[20] They extended Feuerbach's search for the natural, the humanistic "species man" into a more detailed study of property relationships and found in the change of these relationships the clue to the "true" man, thus becoming known as "true socialists." They were a rather easy-going set of pleasant individuals with literary leanings, respectful of Hess and Feuerbach and somewhat in awe of Marx and Engels. Their typical representative was Dr. Karl Grün (1817–87), the author of a popularly written book on socialism in France and Belgium, (1845), which contained entertaining accounts of his conversations with Considérant, Proudhon and other socialist leaders.

Marx and Engels were far from impressed by these "true socialists." "They think that they have performed miracles when they translate statements which already have become trivialities into the language of Hegel's logic and send this newly acquired wisdom into the world as something yet unheard of as the "true German theory" wrote Engels in 1845.[21] This German belletristic socialism, which neither possessed the profundity of Marx's and Engels' thought, nor demanded the self-sacrificing devotion of these men and of Hess and Weitling, reflected the indecision typical of the German intellectual middle class as a whole. Yet neither Marx nor Engels ever broke their ties with them as absolutely as might be inferred from some of their utterances. One of the "true socialist" papers, the Westphälisches Dampfboot— Steam Boat of Westphalia—even printed Marx's merciless critique of one of Grün's books. Marx and Engels were hoping to win some of them over to their camp. And indeed, at least one, Weydemeyer, became a close associate.

"True socialism," like Young Hegelianism as a whole, is now hardly ever remembered except as the subject of a spirited polemical section in the Communist Manifesto. It disappeared after 1848.

III. MARX AND ENGELS

Marx and I were pretty much the only people to rescue conscious dialectics from German idealistic philosophy and apply it to the materialistic conception of nature and history.

—Engels, Preface to *Anti-Dühring*, 1885

When we assume a definite stage of the development of production, commerce and consumption, then you have a corresponding social order, a corresponding organization of the family, of the estates or of the classes, in one word, a corresponding civil society. Assume such a society, and you obtain a corresponding political order which is only the official expression of such a society. . . . It is hardly necessary to add that men do not select freely their *productive forces*—the foundation of their entire history—since every productive force is an acquired force, the product of previous activity.

—Marx to P. W. Annenkov, Dec. 28, 1846

1.

Karl Marx, born May 5, 1818 at Trier (Trèves) in the Rhineland, was the son of a well respected lawyer of liberal views. He had a good secondary education, was a voracious reader with a passion for real understanding of what he was reading. To be radical, he once said, is to grasp the things at their roots. In this sense he was a radical from his earliest student days.

At Berlin he studied law, history and philosophy, and joined the Young Hegelians, whose mentors were the Bauers and Ruge, and whose democratic views he shared. In 1841 he received his doctor's degree at Jena on a thesis dealing with ancient Greek materialism.

Finding it impossible to obtain an academic position without sacrificing his political views, Marx became an editor of the bourgeois-democratic *Rheinische Zeitung* in Cologne. He attacked the still powerful feudal interests, parliamentary servility and press censorship. This bitter struggle in the arena of practical democratic politics was fast driving from Marx's brain whatever academic cobwebs Hegelianism had left. When in 1843 censorship killed the paper, Marx was ready not only for Feuerbach but also for socialism.

To seek further understanding of socialism and the revolutionary movement Marx went to Paris, where he arrived in November 1843. Here he published, together with Ruge, a periodical called the *Deutsch-Französische Jahrbücher* (German-French Annals). Only one issue appeared, but it is of importance because it is the first publication in which Marx and Engels gave notice of their communist views.

Frederick Engels, born November 20, 1820, at Barmen, also in the Rhineland, was the son of a textile manufacturer of orthodox Protestant views. He had a good secondary education, became a clerk in a Bremen mercantile house, and shared for a while the romantic patriotism of Young Germany. When in Berlin during 1841–42 in military service, he got in touch with the Young Hegelians and became a radical democrat. From 1843 to 1845 he was in Manchester as an employee in his father's firm. Here he joined the Chartists and studied political economy; through these experiences, plus perusal of Feuerbach's critique of Hegelianism, he became a communist. Hess, at that time, also had some influence on him. As he wrote many years later:

In Manchester it was put right under my nose that economic facts, which so far have played no role or a negligible one in the writing of history, are at least in the modern world a decisive historical force. They form the basis for the origin of the present-day class antagonisms, and these antagonisms are in turn the basis of the formation of political parties and their struggles and thus of all political history.

When, in August 1844, on a visit to Paris, Engels met Marx, the two young men found that along quite different roads they had come to the same conclusions.

The papers that Marx and Engels wrote for the *Annals* contain their new outlook, but still only in the broadest outline. In a critique of Hegel's philosophy of law Marx pointed to the revolutionary role of the new class, the proletariat, as the carrier of the social revolution, the class that can and must abolish private property. It could accomplish this historic task only if guided by a theory, which would be the final development of German philosophy:

> As philosophy finds its *material* weapon in the proletariat, so the proletariat finds its *intellectual* weapons in philosophy. . . .
> The head of this emancipation is philosophy, its heart the proletariat.

Engels' contributions to the Annals include a critique of British political economy and an account of the class struggles of the British working class, both of great help to Marx. Marx also studied the French Revolution and political economy, and continued his critique of Hegel in the light of his understanding of the class struggle. Much of his thought was laid down in papers published only in recent years under the title of *Economic and Political Manuscripts of 1844*.[1] They analyze the alienation of man from his fellow man, from the products of his labor and from himself under the influence of the capitalist system of exploitation. Only the abolition of private property could destroy this alienation. This, Marx insisted, was the true interpretation of Hegel's search for freedom. Already in this early work as a communist Marx's critique of society showed a depth not reached by any socialist writer up to that time.

Marx also stayed in close contact with the French working class movement and with the German societies of radical artisans. He did not join them, since their confused communism, a mixture of Babeuf, Blanqui, Lamennais and Weitling, did not appeal to him. He knew many leading radicals personally, spent many hours with Proudhon and with the German poet Heinrich Heine, a radical democrat who was living in Paris in self-imposed political exile and who in this period wrote some of his most stirring political poems. He was also very well informed on

French art and politics, and his astute and witty introduction to German philosophy remains a treat.

When Marx and Engels met in August 1844, they got along so well that they decided on collaboration; their classical friendship began in that month. By the time Engels left for home they had already started on their first joint venture, a critique of Bauer's brand of Hegelianism. It appeared in 1845 as *Die Heilige Familie*—The Holy Family. Much of it is dated, but it contains, among other gems, Marx's brilliant exposition of British and French materialism.[2]

Marx found an outlet for his political writing in the German language paper *Vorwärts*, published in Paris. One of his articles dealt with the revolt of the Silesian textile workers, where he came into sharp conflict with Ruge. Marx saw in the strike the beginning of the emancipation of the German proletariat, its "gigantic children's shoes;" Ruge, who always remained a bourgeois democrat, considered it unimportant. But when the Vorwärts continued to attack the miserable political conditions in Germany, the Prussian government took steps and complained to the French. The Guizot government obliged, and as one of its measures forced Marx to leave France, together with Ruge and Bakunin.[3] Marx settled in Brussels, where many European radicals had gathered. Engels joined him shortly thereafter.

2.

Marx's stay in Brussels (1845–48) was of vital importance in the development of European thought. It was here that Marxism obtained its definite form, fully emancipated from Hegel's idealism and Feuerbach's abstract materialism. This period also marks the beginning of organized Marxist-inspired political action—the beginning of a communist movement in the modern sense.

Engels finished his book *Die Lage der arbeitenden Klassen in England*—The Condition of the Working Classes in England— still a model of labor research, but of research with a historical perspective, leading to a militant conclusion. He also collaborated with Marx on a book intended as a final settling of accounts with Feuerbach, the Young Hegelians and the dilettantic socialists among them. It became a voluminous opus, but it failed to find a publisher, so that it was left to the "gnawing criticism of the mice." After all, as Engels said in retrospect, the work had accomplished what above all they had set out to reach: self-clarification. The manuscript was finally saved from the mice by the Russians, and it appeared in 1932 as *Die Deutsche Ideologie,* The German Ideology.[4]

Most of this book, especially Part II, is, like most of *The Holy Family,* too topical and discursive to be of much use today. At the same time, Parts I and III contain a wealth of brilliant passages of lasting importance. Here, for the first time, Marx and Engels passed their considered judgment on Feuerbach and formulated what became known as historical materialism, the method based on the proposition that "the mode of production in material life determines the general character of the social, political and spiritual processes of life," and that "it is not the consciousness of men that determines their existence, on the contrary, their social existence determines their consciousness," as Marx formulated it later.[5] Their conclusion about Feuerbach's abstract materialism was epitomized in the words: "In so far as Feuerbach is a materialist, there is no history to him, and in so far as he considers history, he is not a materialist."[6]

Still another statement points out that "The ideas of the ruling class are in every epoch the ruling ideas, that is: the class which is the ruling *material* force in society, is at the same time the ruling *intellectual* force."[7]

In the same period Marx also wrote his famous *"Theses on Feuerbach"*—as answer to Feuerbach's *Thesen* of 1842—formulating the basic principles of dialectical materialism and ending with the much quoted statement, "The philosophers have *interpreted* the world in various ways; the point however is to *change* it."[8]

Marx's studies at that time centered on economics, and he began to develop the critical analysis that would eventually lead to *Capital.* He brought his understanding to good use when, after he and Engels had clarified their position with respect to German socialism, he did the same with regard to its French counterpart. Here the most important thinker was Proudhon, who in an answer to a letter of Marx, written in 1846, had refused to collaborate with him in his revolutionary activity. Marx's answer was his *Misère de la philosophie,* directed against Proudhon's latest work, the *Philosophie de la misère.* The book, written in French, appeared in 1847. It is the first published book in which Marx developed historical materialism and explained the results he had reached in his critique of political economy. To use a phrase of Lassalle, Marx shows himself a Ricardo turned socialist and a Hegel turned economist. The book culminates in a spirited defense of trade unions and their strikes—activities Proudhon opposed.

The literary activity of Marx and Engels included the publication of a spate of articles and essays in papers and periodicals with a radical democratic tendency, published in Belgium, Germany, France and England. Marx also gave lectures, and out of a series, given in 1847 to the recently founded German Workers Society, came his pamphlet *Lohnarbeit und Kapital*—Wage-Labor and Capital[9]—the first popularly written exposition of Marxian economics.

3.

Marx and Engels worked in a heavily charged political atmosphere. With the revival of the radical movement after 1840 it was clear that a storm was rising over Europe. The revolutionary spirit was quickened in all parts. An economic crisis was brewing, and actually occurred in 1846–47, accompanied by abject misery and rising resistance. In France the monarchy became more and more discredited, opposition was growing; in England Chartism was moving masses of workers. In Switzerland the *Sonderbund* war saw the bourgeois cantons lined up against the cantons where the old aristocracy reigned basing itself on an archaic peasant economy. In 1846 the Rebellion in Cracow, accompanied by other outbreaks in Poland, raised high hopes, followed by deep resentment when the rebellion was shattered by the Tsar's bloody suppression. In Prussia, in 1847, the king was at last compelled to call together the Diet to balance his budget, a task which could be accomplished only with the support of the reluctant bourgeoisie. This circumstance stirred up memories of 1789, when Louis XVI had been forced to call together the Estates General—and even of Charles I and the Long Parliament. As Engels wrote in January 1848, at the time Marx and he were finishing the *Communist Manifesto:*

The year 1847 was certainly the most agitated one for a long time. In Prussia a constitution and a United Diet, in Italy an unexpectedly quick awakening of political life, and a general call to arms against Austria, in Switzerland a civil war, in England a new parliament with a definitely radical color, in France scandals and reform banquets, in America the conquest of Mexico by the United States—that is a sequence of changes and movements such as we have not seen in recent years.[10]

The position taken by Marx and Engels in regard to the revolutionary struggles ahead was based on their understanding that the growth, political awakening and final emancipation of the working class could proceed faster and more effectively under a bourgeois-democratic than under a feudalistic-autocratic regime. The examples of Great Britain and France with their political parties and relative freedom of the press, the first with its Chartist movement, the second with its lively socialist agitation, as against that of Germany with its lack of political life, its censorship and retarded economic growth lent overwhelming weight to this position. The task of German communists was first of all to destroy all remnants of feudalism, so that in this respect the bourgeoisie and the working class had a common interest. The working class had to press the bourgeoisie to overcome its timidity and cowardice. Once a bourgeois-democratic regime was established, the working class should struggle for its revolutionary replacement by a workers' republic.

This position, based on an analysis of the realities of their time, placed Marx and Engels in opposition to many "true socialists," who, led by abstract reasoning based on Hegel and

Feuerbach, only wanted to work for an immediate socialist revolution. They claimed that neither they nor the workers had any interest in a bourgeois revolution, which would result in the victory of the direct enemy of the working class. This position could serve only reaction, and the Prussian government actually used "true socialist" arguments to convince the workers that feudal reaction was their true ally against the bourgeoisie.

Their position also pitted Marx and Engels against other trends then popular in the socialist movement, such as those influenced by Proudhon, Cabet or the disciples of Fourier. Then there were the radical democrats who struggled for the bourgeois revolution but feared its extension into the revolution of the proletariat.

The time had come to bring the left together and to propagate the new realistic approach to communism. Marx and Engels, working in Brussels, gathered around them a group of radicals of similar mind, some native Belgians, others voluntary or proscribed exiles. A trip of several weeks in the summer of 1845 to England enabled them to become acquainted or renew acquaintance with some of the revolutionaries in the country, notably with left-wing Chartists like Harney and with members of the League of the Just residing in London, mostly Germans, headed by the intelligent triumvirate—Schapper, Moll and Bauer. These radicals of different tendencies were ready to be brought together; later in that same year we have that memorable Feast of the Nations in London and the organization of the Fraternal Democrats, described previously. Encouraged by these and other developments Marx and Engels, back in Brussels, launched early in 1846 a Communist Correspondence Committee to bring different groups of communists and sympathizers in Europe and America closer together, to inform them about what was happening in different countries and to prepare for the formation of a communist action group. Some of their most important contacts were with the London leaders of the League of the Just and with left Chartists. Harney as well as the leaders of the Just expressed their willingness to serve as the London representatives of the Correspondence Committee, despite still existing differences with the position taken by Marx and Engels.

The Brussels Committee was strengthened by the arrival of Wilhelm Wolff (1809–64), a former Breslau teacher, son of a Silesian peasant and a revolutionary fighter who had spent five years in Prussian prisons. Nicknamed Lupus, he became one of Marx's closest friends, and joined him later in England; it was to his memory that Marx dedicated the first volume of *Capital*. The Correspondence Committee also established relations with individuals and groups in Germany, where Weydemeyer in Westphalia was one of the most faithful friends. Hess was sympathetic and collaborative. Attempts were made to establish contacts in Switzerland and also in Paris. As headquarters of the League of the Just, Paris was particularly important; Engels moved from Brussels to Paris for the work of conversion.

We do not know too much about the work of the Committee, as is the case with so many other revolutionary activities in history, which because of the police have to be carried out by word of mouth or private letter rather than in print. We do know that the Committee sent out, apart from letters, lithographed and printed messages, some of which have been preserved. For instance, we possess three reports from Paris to the Brussels Committee from Engels, dated September and October 1846, in which he described his efforts to propagate his ideas among the German artisans influenced by Proudhon, Weitling and Grün. Here he stressed the intentions of the communists as follows: (1) to work in the interests of the proletarians in opposition to those of the bourgeois, (2) to achieve this by abolition of private property and its replacement by the community of goods, (3) to recognize no other means to accomplish this than the violent, democratic revolution.[11] This was, of course, not the whole of the program, but that aspect of it which Engels emphasized.

However, the most important practical achievement of the Committee was its influence on the London League of the Just.

4.

The League of the Just had been founded at Paris in 1836 among those German workers and intellectuals who had come under the spell of current socialist and communist ideas. It was in part a propaganda club, partly a secret society. It recruited its members mainly from apprentices and artisans, often still petty-bourgeois in their outlook, but already proletarian in their way of life. Many had eked out a precarious existence traveling from one place to another, a life of great uncertainty and hardship, but which also tended to broaden their political horizon. It made them into propagandists for the League when they trekked from place to place, even penetrating the police barrier set up inside Germany. Their usual method was to join or form workers' societies for open educational and social purposes—*Arbeiterbildungsvereine*—and use them as recruiting grounds for the League. Headquarters were in Paris, where, as we have seen, Weitling played a leading and more and more prophetic role. His book of 1838, *Humanity as It Is and as It Should Be,* with its confused religious utopian but also militant revolutionary teachings, served as a kind of official program.

The Paris branches of the League participated in the abortive insurrection of 1839 led by Blanqui's Seasons. The persecution that followed at first disorganized the League, but not for long. During its recovery under Weitling's leadership, it continued its activities abroad, especially in England, Germany and Switzerland. Weitling himself set off for Geneva in 1841, where he agitated with his usual indomitable fervor and wrote his principal work, the *Guaranties.* He was thrown in prison and after his release went via Germany to London, where he arrived in 1845 to find a flourishing branch of the League of the Just.

This branch was headed by Karl Schapper and his friends Joseph Moll and Heinrich Bauer. Schapper (1812–70), a former student of forestry, exiled from Germany and Switzerland because of revolutionary activities, was now a typesetter, "in shape a giant, resolute and energetic, always ready to sacrifice bourgeois existence and life," as Engels later reminisced. In London he met Joseph Moll (1812–49), a watchmaker, "a medium-sized Hercules," who became the diplomat of the group. They were instrumental in founding the *Deutsche Arbeiterbildungsverein*—the German Workers Educational Society—often to be called the Communist Workers Educational Society. Additional strength came in 1842 from Heinrich Bauer, who had first worked on the Paris reorganization of the Just—a cobbler, "a vivid, happy, witty little man whose small frame held a fund of shrewdness and determination," as Engels described him.[12]

The Educational Society was an open social club, vital enough to survive until World War I.[13] Following the common practice of the Just, Schapper and his friends organized their League as a secret club among the members of this society. Secrecy was hardly necessary so far as England itself was concerned, but the League had to protect its connections on the continent and, after all, England had also its sorry stable of informers. Secrecy did not prevent Engels from getting in touch with the League, perhaps through Harney. This must have been the first time the young and sensitive textile clerk met German revolutionary workers. They made a deep and lasting impression on him, these "three true men," as he expressed himself many years later. But he did not join the League, dissatisfied with its unclear Weitling-Fourier-Proudhon-Babeuf inspired program of egalitarianism, which did not see the importance of the class struggle. Marx in Paris had behaved in the same way with respect to the Just and other secret groups in that capital.

In the British political atmosphere, so much freer than on the continent, the London Just lost a good deal of their inherited provincialism and revolutionary romanticism, especially through their contact with the trade union movement and the Chartists. Internationalists from the beginning (the League had members of many nationalities, who conversed in German as the common language), they participated with the British in the Feast of the Nations and in the Fraternal Democrats. The Feast of the Nations was addressed not only by Harney (toast to the French revolution), but also by Weitling, then visiting London after being expelled from Switzerland (toast to pledge the international brotherhood of all democrats). Engels, at that time (September 1845) in Germany, reported enthusiastically on this meeting in a German periodical and concluded, rather over-optimistically perhaps: "Is it not true when I say that in these days democracy is communism?"[14]

It was with these London Just that Marx and Engels in 1846 established their communist correspondence. One of the obstacles they had to overcome was a kind of anti-intellectualism among revolutionary artisans, a distrust not of knowledge as such (many of them were ardent readers of all kinds of worthwhile literature, about Cleopatra, the Reformation and prostitution, not to speak of Owen, Cabet and Feuerbach) but of college graduates and their *Gelehrtenarroganz,* their scholar's arrogance. Universities were—and still are—bulwarks of the ruling class. Such an attitude has never disappeared from the labor movement, nor for that matter, has its counterpart among intellectuals, although there are excellent examples to the contrary. Weitling was such an anti-intellectualist. But around 1845–46 Schapper and his comrades began to tire of their great leader who had appeared among them in person during 1845, of his messianism, his superficial egalitarianism and constant repetition of the same phrases. Weitling, as a matter of fact, had reached the end of his intellectual growth. Did he feel that he had outlasted his welcome?

At any rate, in March 1846 we find him in Brussels, where he was cordially received by Marx and his communist group, then discussing the tactics for Germany. But soon differences of opinion crept in and already in the same month there was a violent clash at one of the group meetings. Marx pressed Weitling for a concrete program for propaganda in Germany. Marx and Engels knew what they wanted; rejecting all utopianism, they urged political organization of the working class to gain full bourgeois democracy before it pressed toward communism. Weitling's reaction to this was negative: he had only generalities to offer, and was furious that he, the poor tailor who had done and sacrificed so much for the workers, was criticized by some bookish and rich (!) young men. But Weitling lost out against Marx's bitingly realistic approach; and shortly afterward, as we have seen, he accepted an invitation to come to the United States. Here he resumed his role as a leader of German artisans, returned for a short time to participate in the German Revolution of 1848, but after his return to America got more and more lost in utopian schemes.

The conflict with Weitling was accompanied by another—with Herman Kriege (1820–1850), a pupil of Feuerbach, a member of the London Just and of the Brussels communist group. Kriege had emigrated in 1845 to New York with the intention to sow the seed of communism among the many German workers residing in America, especially in New York. Kriege turned out to be a disappointment: he conducted his propaganda in the worst "true socialist" manner, so that the Brussels group in May 1846, (Weitling dissenting) found it imperative to issue a sharp protest against Kriege's "fantastic emotional fervor" *(phantastische Gemütsschwärmerei).*[15] This necessary clarification of principles added to the conflict with "true socialism" as a whole. It also involved Hess who often worked closely with Marx and Engels—or at any rate tried to—but constantly vacillated between his Young Hegelian abstract search for the "true" society and Marxian historical materialism.

We mention these conflicts not only because they reveal some of the birthpangs of scientific socialism, but also because it is not uncommon to find commentators on Marxism, even friendly ones, talking of Marx as of some Jewish or Christian Messiah, attributing to him all kinds of vague prophetic ideas about the communist future. This is confusing Marx with Weitling or Hess. We must stress how sharply Marx drew the line between himself and Engels on the one hand and Weitling and Hess on the other, without, it must be added, falling into the pitfall of sectarianism. They were always willing to join hands with those democrats who fought actively for the emancipation of the working masses.

After the organization of the Brussels Correspondence Committee with its contacts in London and Germany the time had come to establish a branch in Paris also. Marx, in May 1846, wrote to Proudhon, asking him to join, but Proudhon politely refused. He had no objection to discussion, he said, but he shrank from revolutionary activity; he may also have resented Marx warning him against his admirer, Karl Grün. This was the end of the friendship with Proudhon. Thus Marx in 1846 had to break with two outstanding working class leaders, both of proletarian origin, Weitling and Proudhon. Both men, doubtlessly endowed with a touch of brilliancy, had participated in the start of the movement and in their time had inspired Marx and Engels. Now they were falling behind, as also was Hess. Weitling stuck to his artisan communism of universal equality, Proudhon to his petty-bourgeois anarchism, and Hess could not make up his mind. They failed to grasp what Marx and Engels saw so clearly now: the revolutionary role of the proletariat, the need to organize it not only for discussion, but for day by day political and economic activity, so that in the course of the actual struggle the proletariat could remake itself for the taking over of power and the building of a new society.

Engels, we have seen, left Brussels for Paris in the summer of 1846 to propagate the ideas of the Communist Correspondence Committee, in the first place among the members of the League of the Just, mostly German tailors and cabinet makers, but also among the French. At that time Karl Grün was in Paris; affable and cultured, he had considerable influence among them. Hess also made appearances and was not always helpful. Engels, who worked hard and talked at many meetings, succeeded in gaining influence over Grün and his associates. He also collaborated with a French group called Social Democrats—perhaps the first time this name appears—with their paper *La Réforme,* edited by the radical democrat Ferdinand Flocon, an admirer of Marx. Engels stayed in Paris until after the February Revolution of 1848, in active correspondence and occasional personal contact with Marx and the Brussels group as well as with the London Just.

5.

Thus Marx and Engels were the leading spirits of a growing international communist group in a Europe rapidly moving into a new revolutionary situation. The group was still very loosely held together and the outlook of the membership was mixed and often confused, with partisans of Weitling, Hess, Fourier, Grün, Blanqui and Proudhon alongside followers of Marx and Engels. It was time for an effort to unify them under a common program. Already in July 1846 the Brussels Committee suggested to its London correspondents that they issue a call for an international congress of communists; that is, they appealed to the League of the Just.[16]

During that year the hands of these London Just had been strenghtened because increased persecution by the Paris police had induced the Paris Just to move the headquarters of the organization to London. From here, in November 1846, the new executive committee did send out a circular letter to the branches of the League, with a call for an international congress to be held in May 1847, to thresh out the different ideas held by the members and to come to some common credo. The committee felt it absolutely necessary to draw in Marx and his friends, despite the fact that neither Marx nor Engels were members of the League.

Consequently, in January 1847, Moll went on a diplomatic mission in the name of the Communist Corresponding Committee in London. First he went to see Marx and Wolff in Brussels, then he looked up Engels in Paris, and invited them to join the League and to participate in the planned conference. They were promised full freedom of expression. Under such circumstances Marx and Engels, who had been looking for a more closely knit and larger international organization than they had so far ("after all, the fellows are a couple of hundred men strong, and are accredited to the English by Harney," Engels had written to Marx in December 1846), and who appreciated the changing outlook in Schapper and his associates, decided to join. Several other members of the Brussels group joined with them, perhaps also Hess.

The London headquarters of the League of the Just now sent out a second call, in February 1847, sounding a more positive note than in the rather vague first call. It held up the Chartist movement as an example to the communists, "who, we are sorry to say, do not yet form a party"—and that in the face of a coming revolution. The opening date of the congress was now set for June 1, 1847.

The congress took place in London, June 2–7. Marx was not present for lack of money. Engels, now a member of the organization, came as representative of the Paris sections, Wolff of the Brussels section. Not much was known about this congress until some documents relating to it were recently discovered in Hamburg.[17] We did know that at this congress the League of the Just shed its conspiratorial character and reorganized on a democratic basis, on what now we would call "democratic centralism," and that it was decided to change the name of the organization to *Bund der Kommunisten,* League of the Communists. We are accustomed to call it the Communist League. We also knew that it was decided to issue a periodical.

Now the statutes drafted at the congress have come to light and the first thing that strikes us is the call to battle which heads the text, *Proletarians of All Countries, Unite!* This is the first time this slogan appears—to replace the former declamations calling in the abstract for justice, equality and brotherhood. We may safely ascribe the introduction of these words at the congress to Engels. The key words from now on were no longer *love for humanity,* but *organization;* no longer *equality,* but *solidarity.*

The statutes themselves, however, show that the Marxian approach was still insufficiently appreciated. Article 1 proclaims: "The League aims at the destruction of man's enslavement [*Entsclavung der Menschen*] by the dissemination of the theory of the community of goods and its practical introduction as soon as possible."

This was clearly a compromise between the different factions. Some of this appears also in the draft "confession of faith" adopted at the conference, to be submitted to the different branches of the League for discussion in preparation of the new congress, scheduled for November of the same year. We now also have a copy of this document, lithographed in Engels' handwriting and signed by Schapper and Moll (under assumed names). It is reproduced in this book in English translation. Although a compromise, it already shows strongly the Marx-Engels influence.

Moreover, we have a report on the congress sent to the membership. We learn from it that the London branch [*Gemeinde*] was the strongest, with possibility of propaganda in several organizations. The Paris branches were weakened because of internal fights against Grün's partisans, but the remaining members showed a new militant spirit. There were members in Lyons and Marseille. The Brussels branch, as we can expect, was very efficient; it had also founded a branch in Liège. As to Germany, the branches in Berlin had been raided by the police, but there were also branches in Hamburg, Bremen, Munich, Leipzig and eight other German cities. In Switzerland the League was weakened because of the Weitling influence and the interference of the police. But there was a branch in Stockholm.

As to the periodical, only one issue appeared, in September 1847, named *Kommunistische Zeitung.* Most of it was written, it seems, by Schapper. It also carries the slogan "Proletarians of All Countries, Unite."[18]

6.

Marx, in Brussels with his group—now a branch of the Communist League—followed the old practice of the Just and organized in August a German Workers Educational Society, of which —not without opposition by "true" and other socialists—he became a vice-president. In July his *Poverty of Philosophy* had appeared, with the first published results of his economics studies, but in French. He now presented his views in German through lectures before the new Society. These lectures, as mentioned before, were later published under the title of *Wage-Labour and Capital.* Marx also had found a local outlet for his journalistic work in the *Deutsch-Brüsseler Zeitung,* the German-Brussels Newspaper. All this, in addition to the fact that Marx and Engels now had in the Communist League an international organization for the dissemination of their ideas, seemed to have made continuation of the Communist Correspondence Committee no longer necessary. At any rate, it disappears from the scene.

Discussions in connection with the proposed "confession of faith" or credo took place in the branches of the League. Through Engels' letters to Brussels, we are well informed about

Paris, where the debates were quite agitated, not only around what was left of Grün's influence, but also around Hess. This faithful, but confused, militant had come from Brussels to Paris, and, now a member of the League, had submitted his own "divinely improved" (gottvoll verbesserte) confession of faith. The qualification is due to Engels, who had to attack it. Hess' draft has not been preserved, but he had already published a confession of faith in 1846 in the form of a catechism, and in 1849–50 he published another, both happily preserved, so that by reading them we can easily understand Engels' opposition.[19] They were in substance emotional appeals for love and against wickedness (represented by money). Historical materialism remained alien to Hess. The upshot was that Engels won out in these debates among the tailors and cabinet makers, so that he obtained a mandate to write his own confession of faith in the name of the Paris Just. This was in October, and during this and the next month he wrote it down, in 25 questions and answers, an improved version of his June draft. He submitted it to Marx with the words:

Think a little about the confession of faith. I believe that the best thing is to do away with the catechism form and give the thing the title: Communist Manifesto. We have to bring in a certain amount of history, and the present form does not lend itself to this very well. I take with me from Paris what I have written; it is a simple narrative, but miserably composed, in an awful hurry . . . (letter of November 23–24, 1847).

This draft by Engels has also been preserved. He called it Grundsätze des Kommunismus and it can be found in this book, entitled "Principles of Communism." It lacks the superb style and grand design of the Manifesto, but it contains many of its leading ideas in that simple form Engels mastered so well. It lacks the compromises of the June draft.

The second congress of the Communist League took place, also in London, from November 29 to December 8, 1847.[20] This time both Marx and Engels were present. The program was the main point on the agenda. There still were violent disagreements and the debates lasted ten days. Marx and Engels had to use their powers of persuasion to the utmost to convince the majority of the correctness of their program. But they won out, and the old idyllic "community of goods" was replaced by the new realistic political-economic program of the class struggle to abolish private property. The new statutes show it. They now proclaimed the task of the League as follows:

> The overthrow of the bourgeoisie, the domination of the proletariat, the abolition of the old bourgeois society based on class antagonisms and the establishment of a new society without classes and without private property.

Marx and Engels in those days always used the term "private property" and not "private property of the means of production". However, if we consider their actual statements, that is what they had in mind above all.

As a result of the debates, the congress gave Marx the task of drawing up the new "confession of faith" as the official program of the League. Marx accepted, and thus came to write the *Communist Manifesto*.

We have no detailed account of the debates at the conference. Instead, we have a picture of Marx and Engels as they appeared at that time, written long afterwards by an old comrade:[21]

> Marx was then still a young man, about 28 years old, but he greatly impressed us all. He was of medium height, broad-shouldered, powerful in build and energetic in his deportment. His brow was high and finely shaped, his hair thick and pitch-black, his gaze piercing. His mouth already had the sarcastic line that his opponents feared so much. Marx was a born leader of the people. His speech was brief, convincing and compelling in its logic. He never said a superfluous word; every sentence was a thought and every thought was a necessary link in the chain of his demonstration. Marx had nothing of the dreamer about him. The more I realized the difference between the communism of Weitling's time and that of the *Communist Manifesto,* the more clearly I saw that Marx represented the manhood of socialist thought.
> Frederick Engels, Marx's spiritual brother, was more of the Germanic type. Slim, agile, with fair hair and mustache, he was more like a smart young lieutenant of the guard than a scholar. . . . He was a man you respected and loved once you knew him intimately.

Marx returned to Brussels, and with Engels' draft, and whatever notes about the conference he had before him, began to write the new program, adopting Engels' suggestions that it be a

Manifesto. He set about it in his usual painstaking way, striving for as perfect a form as possible. It took him so much time that Schapper and his friends grew impatient and on January 24, 1848, sent him a kind of ultimatum: "that if the Manifesto . . . does not reach London before Tuesday, February 1, further measures will be taken." This angry missive strikes us as mildly ludicrous, to say the least, knowing, as we know now, the masterpiece coming from Marx's pen at the time. But the guns of the revolution were already blasting in Milan and Palermo, and the comrades were in a hurry to obtain their program.

Marx completed his manifesto early in February 1848. The manuscript was sent to London, where it was immediately brought to the printer, in a little shop in Bishopsgate.[22] The *Manifest der Kommunistischen Partei,* now known as the *Communist Manifesto,* was published as the official program of the Communist League in mid-February. A few days later the revolution came to Paris, and from there spread over Europe.

IV. THE COMMUNIST MANIFESTO

. . . That is the line of action [first laid down in the *Communist Manifesto*] which the great founder of modern socialism, Karl Marx, and with him, I and the Socialists of all nations who worked along with us, have followed for more than forty years, with the result that it has led to victory everywhere, and that at this moment the mass of European socialists . . . are fighting as one common army under one and the same flag.

—Engels, Preface to *The Condition of the Working Classes in England*, 1887

In this work the new world outlook is sketched with the clarity and expressive power of genius: the consistent materialism which also embraces the domain of social life, the dialectic as the most comprehensive and most profound theory of development, the theory of the class struggle and the world historical revolutionary role of the proletariat, the creator of the new, the communist society.

—Lenin, *Karl Marx*, 1914.

1.

The *Manifesto* is divided into four sections. The first, opening with the classical statement: "The history of all hitherto existing society is the history of class struggles," sketches in perspective the revolutionary rise of the bourgeoisie on the ruins of the feudal system. It shows how the powerful productive forces unleashed by the bourgeoisie are approaching a level where they are no longer compatible with the existing property relations. The proletariat, the class the bourgeoisie itself has created, is the new revolutionary class which alone can control and further develop the forces of modern technology. But whereas the triumph of the bourgeoisie over the feudal classes is still the replacement of one exploiting minority by another, the victory of the proletariat in the class struggle is bound to end the exploitation of man by man.

The second section explains the role of the communists as the most advanced and resolute section of the working class. They have the advantage of a theory illuminating the course of the proletarian movement toward the revolution. The text clarifies the actual goals of the communists and heaps scorn on the objections raised against their program.

The third section takes issue with other existing schools of socialist thought, the reactionaries, the utopians and the humbugs. Thus it clarifies communist principles in another way. These three sections are at the same time a lesson in revolutionary dialectics and in the application of historical materialism to social change.

The fourth section, now dated but still of more than historic interest, is a brief exposition of the position of the communists in regard to other radical democratic movements. The attitude is non-sectarian: All movements with a genuine democratic content are to be supported, although the communists should not lose their identity as a motive force toward a proletarian revolution. The main interest is centered on Germany, since the impending bourgeois revolution in that country was seen as the prelude to a proletarian revolution. The final words proclaim that the communists refuse to be a conspiratorial sect and openly declare that their goal is the proletarian revolution. Hence their appeal: "Proletarians of All Countries, Unite!"

2.

Much has been written about the sources of the ideas advanced in the *Manifesto*. How far were they original? Our introduction has shown, we hope, the essential character of Marx's contribution. Yet it is only natural that, as in the case of all great historical documents, the *Manifesto* owes much to previous writings, even though the brilliant and creative synthesis is all Marx's.

It is true that Babeuf had already envisioned the final struggle between the large majority of the dispossessed and the tiny minority of the rich. Saint-Simon had been aware of progressive development in society and of the impact of science and technology. He and many other utopians had analyzed successfully the nature of bourgeois society. Owen had been deeply influenced by modern industrial society and its class character. The class conflict was central to the theories of both British socialists and economists. French historians had come close to the understanding of the British and French Revolutions as class struggles. Blanqui had preached the revolution of the workers and anticipated the concept of the dictatorship of the proletariat (a term not yet used in the *Manifesto,* which, incidentally, does not use the term capitalism either). Elements of historical materialism can be found in the writings of many thinkers of the period. Yet neither all such "borrowings" nor Marx's debt to Hegel and Feuerbach can detract from the originality of the *Manifesto.* This is the reason that it is alive, and that all previous catechisms, confessions of faith and manifestoes have been forgotten.

It is true also that Marx had before him (apart from his notes on the London Congress) Engels' draft, his catechism. But Engels has stressed over and over again his overall indebtedness to Marx.

Several critics have either charged or implied that, in Harold Laski's words, the *Manifesto* "owes much, clearly, to Considérant's *Manifesto of Democracy,* published in 1843 and reprinted in 1847."[1] Others have even claimed direct plagiarism.[2] If this were so, it is strange that Considérant, who lived until 1893, never claimed his paternity. Admittedly, Considérant's indictment of bourgeois society, like other socialists, was both eloquent and penetrating, and he predicted revolutions should the polarization of society into two classes not be arrested. But he missed the main point, the discovery that society changes as the mode of production changes. Furthermore, living under the speculative financial capitalism of the July monarchy, he saw the remedy in the reorganization of the credit system. He remained a utopian; his concept of the future was class harmony based on a rational development of humanity, not the class struggle as the motive force in history. Considérant feared the proletarian revolution, Marx welcomed it. Where Marx called on all proletarians to unite, Considérant exclaimed: "Our cause is the cause of God and of Humanity; our Banner that of Justice, of World Peace and of the Association of Peoples." Noble sentiments, without doubt, but not Marxism. No wonder a recent anti-communist commentator has sighed: "If only Marx had borrowed from Considérant!"[3]

Marx and Engels never denied their indebtedness to their predecessors. We remember how warmly Engels wrote about the great utopians. Marx, in his economic writings, discussed with respect Smith, Ricardo and other economists, as well as Bray and other serious critics of capitalist society—at the same time analyzing and correcting what he saw as their inadequacies. In his letter to Weydemeyer of March 5, 1852, Marx himself clarified this issue of borrowing: "As far as I am concerned, I cannot claim the honor of having discovered the existence either of classes in modern society or of the struggle between them. Bourgeois historians a long time before me have established the historical development of this class struggle, and bourgeois economists its economic anatomy."

And then he stated explicitly what was new on his part. He had shown:

(1) that the *existence of classes* is bound to *definite historical phases of the development of production,*

(2) that the class struggle necessarily leads to the *dictatorship of the proletariat,* and

(3) that this dictatorship is itself only a transition to the *abolition of all classes* and leads to a *classless society.*

Lenin, who quotes this statement, remarks that "in these words Marx has succeeded in expressing with striking clarity, firstly, the chief and concrete differences between his teachings and those of the most advanced and profound thinkers of the bourgeoisie, and secondly, the essence of his teachings concerning the state."[4]

Lenin then continues by pointing out that it is not correct to say that the main point in Marx's teaching is the class struggle.

This had been taught before by bourgeois and utopians, and is even, generally speaking, acceptable to the bourgeoisie. What Marx taught was that the acceptance of the class struggle should be extended to that of the dictatorship of the proletariat. This, he wrote, is the supreme lesson taught by the *Communist Manifesto*.

3.

Whatever the historical antecedents of the *Manifesto* may have been, it is more important to study it in the light of its influence on the world during the span of over a century. Its history had indeed become a part of the history of the labor movement. When it appeared, in 1848, it was received, and enthusiastically received, by only a very small group of militants. The entire Communist League did not count much more than a few hundred members spread over a few cities in Western and Central Europe. They passed the document around in the different languages in which it was issued. Engels mentions a French translation of 1848, which cannot now be traced; he also mentions a Polish translation published in London around the same time, and a Danish one. Harney published an English translation in 1850, noting that it was "written by Citizens Charles Marx and Frederic Engels," the first time the names of the authors were mentioned. But the decline of the movement after the defeat of the revolutions of 1848 also meant the decline of the influence of the *Manifesto*. For years it passed unnoticed, except for two Prussian policemen who included it among their documents on "communist conspiracies."[5] Bourgeois academicians, who could have been inspired by it in their professional studies, flatly ignored it. We do not find any new interest until 1869, when the Russian translation by Bakunin appeared in Switzerland.

Interest in the *Manifesto* awakened after the Paris Commune. In 1871, according to Engels, at least three translations appeared in the United States. From one of them a French translation was published in 1872. In that year there was also a new edition of the original text in Germany, with a preface by Marx and Engels. The now steadily growing international labor movement with its trade unions and socialist parties inspired an equally growing interest in the *Manifesto*. The number of new editions and translations grew apace. We only mention the Russian one of 1882, prepared by G. V. Plekhanov, the "father" of Russian Marxism, the third German edition of 1883 and the English edition of 1888 with the famous preface by Engels. By this time bourgeois academicians at last began to notice the *Manifesto*, if only to decry it. Since those days it has been published in many languages again and again, in millions of copies.[6] There is no other example of a document that, appealing to man's power to change the world, has so affected the lives of uncounted millions. It has been the guiding light in the transformation of society, which has now brought socialism to 14 countries on three continents.

The *Manifesto* has been praised and denounced, analyzed and criticized, seriously as well as facetiously. The most important amendments have been made by Marx and Engels themselves. They were adept at self-criticism, at learning from experience. Immediately after the publication of the *Manifesto* they learned their lesson in the hard school of revolution itself. At first its pattern seemed to conform to their previous analysis. Then came the collapse of Chartism in England, the June (1848) massacre of the protesting workers in Paris, the indecision of the German bourgeoisie, the gradual growth in strength of French and German reaction, the military intervention of the Tsar in Hungary. Clearly, the time for the proletarian revolution had as yet not come. The communists had made too sketchy a parallel between the forms taken by the bourgeois and proletarian revolutions. It is said that generals tend to think in terms of the previous war. In the same way revolutionaries tend to think in terms of previous revolutions. Engels expressed it in 1895:

All of us, as far as our conceptions of the conditions and the course of revolutionary movements were concerned, were under the spell of previous historical experience, particularly that of France. It was, indeed, the latter which had dominated the whole of European history since 1789, and from which now once again the signal had gone forth for general revolutionary change. It was, therefore, natural and unavoidable that our conception of the nature and the course of the "social" revolution proclaimed in Paris in February 1848, of the revolution of the proletariat, should be strongly colored by the memories of the prototypes of 1789 and 1830.

And he concluded that history "has not merely dispelled the erroneous notions we then held; it has also completely transformed the conditions under which the proletariat has to fight. The mode of struggle of 1848 is today obsolete in every respect."[7]

Marx, in his epilogue on the revolution of 1848, written in 1851, had already drawn his conclusions in classical style:

Bourgeois revolutions, like those of the eighteenth century, storm swiftly from success to success; their dramatic effects outdo each other; men and things seem set in sparkling brilliants; ecstacy is the everyday spirit; but they are short-lived; soon they have attained their zenith, and a long crapulent depression lays hold of society before it learns soberly to assimilate the results of its storm-and-stress period. On the other hand, proletarian revolutions, like those of the nineteenth century, criticize themselves constantly, interrupt themselves continually in their own course, come back to the apparently accomplished in order to begin it afresh, deride with unmerciful thoroughness the inadequacies, weaknesses and paltrinesses of their first attempts, seem to throw down their adversary only in order that he may draw new strength from the earth and rise again, more gigantic, before them, recoil ever and anon from the indefinite prodigiousness of their own aims, until the situation has been created which makes all turning back impossible, and the conditions themselves cry out: "Here is Rhodus, leap here!"[8]

What should have happened and what did happen in these revolutionary years of 1848 and 1849 became a subject of heated debate among the defeated revolutionaries. Marx and Engels, after their expectation that the revolution would flare up again had not been realized, came during 1850 to the conclusion that for the time being the revolutionary wave had passed. They began to analyze carefully why it had passed, why capitalism had proved so much stronger than they had expected (for instance, through the discovery of gold in California). They did not share the dreams of many of their comrades in exile, who still were planning new revolutions. Their careful analysis of the situation warned them against adventures of an essentially Blanquist character doomed to failure. These differences were among the causes for the demise of the Communist League, which went out of existence in November 1852.

Critics, with the proud superiority of hindsight, like to smile about Marx's and Engels' expectations of 1848 that the proletarian revolution was "just around the corner." Truth is that even they could not see all the possibilities latent in the capitalism of their day. But they were always willing to learn, always on the alert.[9] It turned out that much of what Marx and Engels expected to happen in their day has come to pass in a longer period of time and then on a larger scale. Their expectations regarding the revolutionary prospect of economically backward Germany in 1847–48 were unrealized, but their general approach was vindicated by the course of the revolution in economically backward Russia of 1917. It is worth quoting what Lenin has written about these errors of Marx and Engels:

Such errors—the errors of the giants of revolutionary thought who tried to raise and did raise the proletariat of the whole world above the level of petty, commonplace and trifling tasks—are a thousand times more noble and magnificent and *historically more valuable and true* than the puerile wisdom of official liberalism, which sings, shouts, appeals, and exhorts about the vanity of revolutionary vanities, the futility of the revolutionary struggle and the charms of counter-revolutionary "constitutional" fantasies.[10]

The Paris Commune of 1871 taught another lesson. Its study led Marx in 1872, in his *Address on the Civil War in France,* to the following vital amendment of the *Manifesto:* "The working class cannot simply lay hold of the ready-made state machinery, and wield it for its own purposes." In the same address he gives an extensive commentary on this statement, tracing the history of the present bourgeois state as "the national power of capital over labor, of public force organized for social enslavement, of an engine of class despotism."[11]

All successful working class revolutionaries, from Lenin to Fidel Castro, have learned this lesson.

Marx returned to the same theme in his *Critique of the Gotha Program,* written in 1875. This work is of the utmost importance since it is the most elaborate programmatic statement that Marx wrote after the *Communist Manifesto*. It offers several amendments to it.

Most importantly, where the *Manifesto* only speaks of the result of the revolution as "the proletariat organized as the ruling class" Marx now is more explicit:

Between capitalist and communist society lies the period of the revolutionary transformation of the one into the other. There corresponds to this also a political transition period in which the state can be nothing but the *revolutionary dictatorship of the proletariat.*

At another place Marx gives his famous division of future society into a first and a higher phase, what we now call the "socialist" and the "communist" stages. The first stage is society

as it *emerges* from capitalist society; which is thus in every respect, economically, morally and intellectually, still stamped with the birthmarks of the old society from whose womb it emerges. Accordingly the individual producer receives back from society—after the deductions have been made—exactly what he gives to it. . . . *Equal right* here is still in principle—*bourgeois right*, although principle and practice are no longer in conflict. . . . The right of the producers is *proportional* to the labor they supply.

But eventually:

In a higher phase of communist society, after the enslaving subordination of individuals under division of labor, and therewith also the antithesis between mental and physical labor, has vanished; after labor, from a mere means of life, has itself become the prime necessity of life . . . only then can the narrow horizon of bourgeois right be fully left behind and society inscribe on its banners: from each according to his ability, to each according to his needs.[12]

Lenin later, in his *State and Revolution,* gave a brilliant commentary on these statements by Marx.

A final amendment to the *Manifesto* can be found in the last preface to this document that Marx and Engels wrote together, for the Russian edition of 1882. Here they pointed out that the time had long passed in which the working class movement had to confine itself, as in 1848, to the West and Central European scene. New situations had arisen requiring new visions. They especially mentioned Russia and the United States. Marx and Engels began to see that the time had come when the struggle would no longer be confined to Western and Central Europe—and anticipated the time when "the Russian revolution will be the signal of a proletarian revolution in the West."

4.

The *Communist Manifesto* is a historic document, to be understood against the political background of the period in which it was written. As early as 1872 Marx and Engels observed that in some respects it was antiquated. At present, with the capitalist system dominated by giant monopolies, and a large section of the earth being transformed from capitalism into socialism, conditions have arisen which the *Manifesto* could only foresee in the most general outline. Why then does the *Manifesto* retain its permanent vitality? How has it stood up during the century and more of its existence?[13]

Marx and Engels, in 1872, were convinced that the general principles laid down in the *Manifesto* were on the whole as correct then as when they were written. Engels, after Marx's death, concurred, since otherwise he would never have consented to the many translations and republications. What then are these general principles?

First, we must mention the method: *historical materialism.* It forms the theoretical backbone of the analysis of capitalism and its origins and of the ways in which proletarian emancipation can be achieved. Its principles are clearly expressed and the subsequent work of Marx and Engels, beginning with their articles of 1848–49 in the *Neue Rheinische Zeitung* and their studies on the class struggles in France and Germany of the period 1848–51, have given us brilliant examples of the power of the method. At present the principles underlying historical materialism not only guide the theoretical and practical work of the millions organized in militant workers' parties over the entire globe, but are accepted in ever widening academic circles.

Secondly, we find in the *Manifesto* the statement that *all history is the history of class struggles.* There still may be moot points in its application to certain periods of the past—for example, the Crusades, where further research may be required. But there is no doubt about the present period. Our whole life is now dominated by the class struggle. What is the Cold War, with the many hot wars that it kindles, but the class struggle raised to a worldwide scale?

Thirdly, the *Manifesto* explains the *nature of capitalism:* commodity production, private ownership of the means of production, accumulation of capital, wage-earning workers, expanding markets and revolutionary subversion of ancient customs and cultures. Capitalism has the class struggle built into the marrow of its bones, and it is this class struggle which eventually leads to its destruction and replacement by a socialist order.

Fourthly, hence we arrive at the necessity and *the historic inevitability of socialism.* Capitalism creates the class which, with all the progress of technology, is not willing to suffer poverty and insecurity or both forever. It creates a militant working class which is compelled and has the capability to establish socialism. The vision of Marx and Engels at a time when the modern working class, except in England, was still in its infancy, is at present being realized in a large section of the earth. The Cold War is a desperate attempt by the ruling capitalist class to prevent the further realization of this vision.

There are other aspects of the *Manifesto* worth mentioning and exploring. We think of its *lack of sectarianism.* Despite, or better, because of its clearcut theoretical and political program, with its sharp criticism of shallow phraseology, even of a "revolutionary" nature, it calls for support of every action of a genuinely democratic nature, be it small or large in scale. We also think of its *rejection of fatalism:* socialism is inevitable, but only because the working class will be forced to will it. In other words, capitalism itself creates the activist mentality of the proletariat: Marx once wrote that in changing nature man changes himself. The same holds for his changing of the social structure.

Finally, there is *the role of the working class parties* guided by Marxian principles. Their task is to give leadership to the emancipation movement of the working masses. Here again the vision of Marx and Engels, whose Communist League of 1847–52 had only a few hundred members, has been turned into a reality on a massive scale. Nowhere has socialism been built except under the leadership of a Marxist workers party, and such parties have been most successful where they were able to express the deepest desires of the working masses, or in the words of the *Manifesto:* where they have shown no interests separate and apart from those of the proletariat as a whole.

5.

A point, often debated, is the way the *Manifesto* deals with nationalism. The statement in Section II that the workers have no fatherland seems to many a gross misunderstanding of the actual situation, or at any rate of the situation as it has since developed. It seems a gratuitous concession to the preachings of Weitling and other socialists of his day. As so often happens a statement taken out of context can be misleading.

It is true that the sentiment expressed in this statement has existed throughout the history of the working class (it was very strong in the IWW, for example; and it is expressed today among many Black militants) . The worker, drawn into the modern capitalist jungle, loses his national, often regional, traits. The peasant, the old-type artisan, the handloom weaver, the worker in small forges, the small townsman, all have a particular affinity to the region in which they are born and bred. Drawn into the factories and mines, severely exploited, they lose their local, even their national, traits as part of the extreme alienation process to which they are subjected. As *The German Ideology* states:

> While the bourgeoisie of each nation still retains its special national interests, big industry creates a class with the same interest among all nations, and among which the nationality has already been destroyed, a class that really has gotten rid of the whole ancient world and at the same time is opposed to it.[14]

But the *Manifesto* does not leave it at that. It sees nationalism as a historic phenomenon. In the course of its emancipation as an oppressed class under the feudal lords to become the ruling

class the bourgeoisie creates the national state for the adminis-
tration of its class interests. Thus the bourgeois concept of nationalism comes into being. But in the struggle of the working
class for its emancipation a new form of nationalism appears. In
its struggle the *Manifesto* says, the proletariat "must rise to be
the leading class of the nation, must constitute itself *the* nation.
It is, so far, itself national, though not in the bourgeois sense of
the word." The *Manifesto* thus sees the struggle of the working
class necessarily in its national context, and in this struggle the
proletariat comes to a new feeling of national belonging. This is
quite different from the nationalism of the bourgeoisie which
prepares the basis for the suppression of other peoples. The proletarian national position is the other side of proletarian internationalism which calls for proletarians of all countries to unite.
The relationship is dialectical.

At another place in the *Manifesto* Marx and Engels expressed
the same idea in another way: "Though not in substance, yet in
form, the struggle of the proletariat with the bourgeoisie is at
first a national struggle. The proletariat of each country must, of
course, first of all settle matters with its own bourgeoisie." Later,
in his critique of Lassalle, whom he saw as conceiving the workers' movement in Germany from a narrow national standpoint,
Marx stressed the word "in form." The substance of the working
class movement was for him and Engels the international aspect.

Marx and Engels were primarily internationalists, not only because they despised the nationalism of the bourgeoisie which
used patriotic phrases to deceive the workers and subordinate
them to its own ends, but also because the struggle of the working class must be based on the mutual support of the workers in
different countries.

For Marx and Engels the national struggle was always seen
from the point of view of the class struggle of the workers. This
determined their position, for example, on the Polish struggle for
liberation. Here was a people suppressed by Russia, Austria and
Prussia. It had rebelled in 1830 and again in 1846. In the heroic
struggle against their oppressors headed by the Tsar the Poles
had gained the sympathy of democrats the world over.

From the beginning Marx and Engels supported the Polish rebellion, especially its left, democratic, wing. This wing was not socialistic; its aim could, in a peasant country, only be the liberation of the peasant from serfdom and the independence of the Polish nation. But Marx and Engels saw this struggle also in its international setting, as an attempt at a serious weakening of Tsarist and Prussian reaction. Thus, at a meeting in London, November 1847, held in commemoration of the Polish rebellion of 1830, Engels having asked to speak as a German, expressed himself as follows:

> We German democrats have a particular interest in the liberation of Poland. The princes who have taken advantage of the partition of Poland were German, the soldiers who even now oppress Galicia and Posen are Germans. We Germans, especially we German democrats, must be especially concerned to wipe this blot from our nation. A nation cannot become free and continue at the same time to oppress other nations.[15]

Engels continued to stress that the liberation of Germany cannot occur without the liberation of the Poles. Here we see Engels as a German patriot, who feels the shame of his country as his own shame, very much like so many Americans at present feel the shame of the Vietnam war as a personal degradation. But Engels' patriotism was part and parcel of his democratic internationalism.

In the Communist League, workers of a number of nations and languages allied themselves in a common cause—and this was a new phenomenon in socialism. Their internationalism had nothing in common with bourgeois cosmopolitanism, which existed then as well as now. The "spirit" of our present international jet-set lived in those days in the circles of free-traders and among certain intellectuals, such as some "true socialists" who from their Hegelian Olympus looked down on "dated" concepts of the nation. Marx and Engels, on the contrary, were deeply aware of the importance of the national struggles for emancipation.

In 1845, Engels, reporting on that London meeting of many nations where Harney and Weitling spoke, addressed himself especially to his "true socialist" readers in Germany:

What do we care about nations? What do we care about the French Republic?

Be quiet, dear Germany. The nations and the French republic do matter very much to us. The fraternisation of the nations, as it is now being accomplished everywhere by the extreme, proletarian, party against the ancient elementary national egoism and the hypocritical, privately egoistic cosmopolitanism of free trade, is more valuable than all German theories on true socialism.[16]

The same principles determined Marx's and Engels' attitude toward Irish liberation. Most Irish lived in abject poverty because of age-old exploitation by their landlords, mostly English, a condition intensified at that time by the potato famine. Irish workers flooded the British labor market and were used by the employers to depress wages—thus setting British labor against Irish labor to the detriment of both.

It was clear that the liberation of Ireland, England's oldest colony, was necessary for the liberation of the British workers. Irish liberation was and remained of paramount importance, and led Marx in 1870 to express it this way: "A people which enslaves another people forges its own chains."[17] Thus Marx and Engels greeted the growing solidarity of British and Irish workers in the Chartist movement:

> We have equally seen with great pleasure the steps taken by the mass of the English Chartists to arrive, at last, at a close alliance between the Irish people and that of Great Britain. We have seen that there is a better chance now than ever before to break down the prejudices which prompted the Irish people to confound in one common hatred the oppressed classes of England with the oppressors of both countries.[18]

We read this in an address signed by three Brussels men, including Marx, to the Fraternal Democrats on February 13, 1848. And shortly before Engels had written in *La Réforme* that this "common alliance between the peoples of the two islands" will have the result that "British democracy . . . shall move forward faster, and poverty stricken Ireland shall at last have made a serious step toward its deliverance."

Thus, the position taken by Marx and Engels relating their democratic internationalism to the various national movements of their time was determined by the needs of the working masses

—workers and peasants—of each country in their class struggle. Neither slogans concerning love nor egalitarian appeals could serve here: each national struggle had to be seen in its historical class setting and judged accordingly. At the same time a clear distinction had to be made between the role of the working masses in the oppressing country—Russia, Prussia or England—and the oppressed country—Poland, Italy or Ireland. No working class in any country could emancipate itself as long as national suppression lasted.

Such an attitude, based on estimation of the concrete current situation, could be influenced by errors of judgment, and it did not always lead to positions that seem correct to us now. An example is Engels' approval of the war of conquest that the United States waged against Mexico in 1846–48—a war opposed by many Americans, including some of the most progressive elements in the United States. In Engels' eye this war had given backward Mexico a chance to participate in the forward historical process under the tutelage of the United States, then the most democratic country in the world—instead of becoming at most a British vassal.[19] He saw, of course, that for the time being only the bourgeoisie would profit; but, in 1848 Marx and Engels thought that only the triumph of the bourgeoisie could lead to the triumph of the working class. In the course of their future career they would test this view critically in various historical settings. Marx and Engels, in contrast to such men as Weitling and Proudhon, were always *learning*.

This may be one of the reasons that later in life they called sections of the *Manifesto* antiquated. They might also have thought of their conviction, expressed in the *Manifesto,* that national differences and antagonisms were on the wane because of the international expansion of capitalist society, the opening of the world market, the growing uniformity of production. But in their willingness to learn and to correct themselves, they took notice of the growth of nationalism and its influence on the labor movement, as when Engels analyzed the way Bismarck utilized the "patriotic hysteria" which accompanied the Franco-Prussian war of 1870.[20] We can also refer to statements in the later prefaces to the *Manifesto,* such as Engels' Preface to the Italian edition of 1893: "Without restoring autonomy and unity to each nation, it would be impossible to achieve the international union of the proletariat, or the peaceful and intelligent cooperation of these nations toward common aims."[21]

Marx and Engels saw deeply into the future, also in their position on national movements. Yet they never lost sight of the fact that proletarian internationalism, always alive even in periods of sweeping nationalism, is the bond that will unite the working masses of the world.

6.

The vibrant actuality of the *Manifesto* lies primarily in its analysis of the nature of capitalism and of the forces leading to its abolition and replacement by socialism—forces capitalism itself brings into being. The present permanent crisis of the capitalist system, the existence of the socialist world and the struggles for national liberation are living proofs of the fundamental correctness of the main thesis of the *Manifesto*. The bourgeoisie has, indeed, created and is still creating its own grave diggers. At the same time we must say with Labriola, that never has a funeral oration been written with such splendor.

The actuality of the *Manifesto* has become so convincing that even in the United States, where for a long time the tender youth of our colleges was protected against the study of this document by the paternal care of the academic authorities, it has now become in many places part of the regular curriculum. The result has been a spate of editions for academic use, and accompanied by introductions, some elucidating, some confusing or worse. We can recommend their analysis to our readers as a useful, and sometimes entertaining, exercise.

One point of academic criticism, however, is worth taking up for a moment. It is the characterization of Marx's method as "economic determinism."[22] Marx was not a determinist, economic or otherwise; his method was that of historical and dialectical materialism. Man, he taught, acts by his own free will, but under circumstances that are historically given. Marxism thus recognizes the role of determinism, but also of indeterminism, both dialectically related. The more we know about nature, about society, about psychology, about history, about ethics, the better can we analyze this relationship. "The method in which real contradictions are resolved," wrote Marx in *Capital*, "is to create the *form* in which they can move."[23] The *Manifesto* teaches how contradictions, such as determinism and free will, nationalism and internationalism, capitalism and socialism are resolved in the historical process.

We sometimes hear that the two last sections of the *Manifesto* are dated beyond repair. This may be true from a narrow historical point of view. We do not hear any more of "true socialists," of Fourierists or Chartists. But, taken in a wider sense, these sections are not so dated as seems at first sight. It appears that our present Left, New as well as Old, still can profit from the critique of the various forms of confused radicalism in the jungle through which the *Manifesto* hacked its way. We still have with us, each in its modern version, our utopians, our petty-bourgeois socialists, our messianists and emotionalists, our men and women who hope that they can come to socialism and brotherhood without the class struggle and without a systematic study of the laws which govern society. We have plenty of quasi-philosophy and phraseology of the "true-socialist" type and the "critical critics" who give, in the struggles for socialism, the intellectuals priority above the working class. And the last section warns especially against one of the cardinal sins of many of the Left, even the Marxian Left, the sin of sectarianism, that splits rather than unites where unity is essential.

Thus the *Manifesto* lives to inspire new generations to clarity of thought and willingness to action, in the struggle for a world free of the exploitation of man by man. The specter of 1848 has taken flesh and has become a glorious reality, retaining its challenge on a worldwide scale. Still the powers of the old and self-styled "free-world" are maintaining their holy alliance to beat the challenger: the Pope and the President, Franco and Sato,

South African racists and American CIA. Still parties in opposition are decried as communistic by their opponents in power, and not a few of them have hurled back that branding reproach at their opponents. But where the *Manifesto* once spoke only for hundreds in a few countries, it now is the voice of millions on all continents.

A barricade at the Cologne Town Hall in Berlin on night of March 18–19, 1848. *Engraving by I. Kirchgov.*

V. MARX AND ENGELS DURING
THE REVOLUTION

1.

During the revolutionary days of February 1848 Marx was in Brussels, Engels in Paris. The Belgian government, afraid that the revolution would descend on Brussels, had Marx arrested—even his wife—and then had him exiled. At that moment Marx received a flattering invitation from Flocon in the name of the revolutionary French government (Louis Philippe had fled and France was a republic): "Tyranny has banished you, free France opens the door to you and to all who struggle for the holy cause of the fraternity of all peoples." Marx went to Paris.

He arrived on March 4. The first task was to reorganize the Central Committee of the Communist League; it now consisted of Marx, Engels and Wolff of the former Brussels League, and of Schapper, Moll and Bauer of the London League. It turned its eye on Germany, where the revolution had started in March, and issued on April 1 a proclamation of 17 points expressing the immediate communist demands for Germany. It deserves attention as expressing Marx's and Engels' ideas for Germany more exactly than the demands of the *Manifesto,* which were the result of a compromise between more divergent groups than those represented on the Paris committee. (A translation appears in the Appendix.) The proclamation demanded a German republic, one and indivisible (observe the terminology of 1792), remuneration of representatives (the Chartist demand), nationalization of feudal property, mines and means of transportation—not of all means of production since the communists wanted to support the bourgeoisie in its conquest of power against the feudal autocracy. The Paris Communist League insistently warned the German militant workers in France against adventurist undertakings, such as forming an emigrant army to invade Germany. The League favored return of revolutionaries to Germany as individuals to associate themselves with local groups in their struggle, and their members followed this advice. Marx and Engels went to the Rhineland, where political freedom was greatest, and there, together with other radicals, they issued the famous daily, the *Neue Rheinische Zeitung*, beginning June 1, 1848. The chief editor was Karl Marx.

From then to May 19, 1849, when it was finally *verboten*, this first communist daily carried its message under Marx's masterful leadership, supported by a brilliant array of other writers, including Engels and such men as the poet Freiligrath. The program of the *Manifesto* was tested on all fronts, domestic and foreign. Appealing to the bourgeoisie to assert the revolutionary task history had bestowed on it, after the model of 1789 and 1792, the paper criticized its failings in the struggle against the autocracy, covered political events as well as economic conditions, warned against pitfalls and gave the militant workers and intellectuals abundant material for agitation and action. It agitated for war against Russia, the bastion of European reaction, a war that could unite Germany as a democracy, just as the war of 1792 had united France. Even now we can learn from it lessons in revolutionary dialectics, and from its brilliant analyses.

The revolution failed and the Prussian government, at last, found the courage to suppress the paper. Defiant to the end, its last number, printed in red, warned the workers in Cologne against provocation. It carried Marx's message to the authorities: "The editors' last word will everywhere and always be: Emancipation of the working classes!" And it also carried the stirring verses of Freiligrath, glorifying "The proud corpse of a rebel":

> No open blow in an open fight,
> By tricks they are doing the slaying—
> I am killed by the rascals that sneak in the night,
> The knaves that the Tsar has been paying[1]

2.

Marx and Engels went to South Germany, still in rebellion, where Engels participated in the armed resistance against the counter-revolutionary forces (in which Moll fell). Marx then went to Paris, where the counter-revolution also was at work, and then in June 1849 settled with his family in London, which would remain his home until his death. Engels joined him in November, and from now on the two friends would act from England in a collaboration which ended only with Marx's death on March 14, 1883. Engels followed him on August 5, 1895.

As to the fate of the Communist League, we can refer to Engels' article (*see* Appendix I). It came to an end in 1852 as a result of the anti-communist trial in Cologne.[2] Many members of the Communist League later played an honorable role in the First International.

PART TWO

MANIFESTO OF
THE COMMUNIST PARTY

(Communist Manifesto)

The text of the Manifesto *is the translation by Samuel Moore, as revised and edited by Frederick Engels for the English edition of 1888, which has become the standard edition. No changes have been made in the text, and the original capitalization is retained. The editor has converted the spelling from English style to American and has made some changes in punctuation where this was required for clarity.*

All footnotes on the page were made by Engels, either to the English edition of 1888 or to the German edition of 1890, as indicated by the year within square brackets at the end of the note. The editor's notes are indicated by superior numbers and will be found at the back of the book.

MANIFESTO OF THE COMMUNIST PARTY

A specter is haunting Europe—the specter of Communism. All the Powers of old Europe have entered into a holy alliance to exorcise this specter: Pope and Tsar, Metternich and Guizot, French Radicals and German police spies.

Where is the party in opposition that has not been decried as Communistic by its opponents in power? Where the Opposition that has not hurled back the branding reproach of Communism against the more advanced opposition parties, as well as against its reactionary adversaries?

Two things result from this fact:

I. Communism is already acknowledged by all European Powers to be itself a Power.

II. It is high time that Communists should openly, in the face of the whole world, publish their views, their aims, their tendencies, and meet this nursery tale of the Specter of Communism with a Manifesto of the party itself.

To this end, Communists of various nationalities have assembled in London and sketched the following Manifesto, to be published in the English, French, German, Italian, Flemish and Danish languages.

The cover of the first edition of the *Communist Manifesto,* published in London in February 1848.

I. BOURGEOIS AND PROLETARIANS*

The history of all hitherto existing society† is the history of class struggles.

Freeman and slave, patrician and plebeian, lord and serf, guild-master‡ and journeyman, in a word, oppressor and oppressed, stood in constant opposition to one another, carried on an uninterrupted, now hidden, now open fight, a fight that each time ended either in a revolutionary reconstitution of society at large or in the common ruin of the contending classes.

In the earlier epochs of history we find almost everywhere a complicated arrangement of society into various orders, a manifold gradation of social rank. In ancient Rome we have patricians, knights, plebeians, slaves; in the Middle Ages, feudal

* By bourgeoisie is meant the class of modern Capitalists, owners of the means of social production and employers of wage labor. By proletariat, the class of modern wage-laborers who, having no means of production of their own, are reduced to selling their labor power in order to live. [*1888*]

† That is, all *written* history. In 1847, the pre-history of society, the social organization existing previous to recorded history, was all but unknown. Since then, Haxthausen discovered common ownership of land in Russia, Maurer proved it to be the social foundation from which all Teutonic races started in history, and by and by village communities were found to be, or to have been, the primitive form of society everywhere from India to Ireland. The inner organization of this primitive Communistic society was laid bare, in its typical form, by Morgan's crowning discovery of the true nature of the *gens* and its relation to the *tribe*. With the dissolution of these primeval communities society begins to be differentiated into separate and finally antagonistic classes. I have attempted to retrace this process of dissolution in: *Der Ursprung der Familie, des Privateigenthums und des Staats*[1], 2nd edition, Stuttgart, 1886. [*1888*]

‡ Guild-master, that is, a full member of a guild, a master within, not a head of a guild. [*1888*]

lords, vassals, guild-masters, journeymen, apprentices, serfs; in almost all of these classes, again, subordinate gradations.

The modern bourgeois society that has sprouted from the ruins of feudal society has not done away with class antagonisms. It has but established new classes, new conditions of oppression, new forms of struggle in place of the old ones.

Our epoch, the epoch of the bourgeoisie, possesses, however, this distinctive feature: it has simplified the class antagonisms. Society as a whole is splitting up more and more into two great hostile camps, into two great classes directly facing each other: Bourgeoisie and Proletariat.

From the serfs of the Middle Ages sprang the chartered burghers of the earliest towns. From these burgesses the first elements of the bourgeoisie were developed.

The discovery of America, the rounding of the Cape, opened up fresh ground for the rising bourgeoisie. The East Indian and Chinese markets, the colonization of America, trade with the colonies, the increase in the means of exchange and in commodities generally, gave to commerce, to navigation, to industry, an impulse never before known, and thereby, to the revolutionary element in the tottering feudal society, a rapid development.

The feudal system of industry, under which industrial production was monopolized by closed guilds, now no longer sufficed for the growing wants of the new markets. The manufacturing system took its place. The guild-masters were pushed on one side by the manufacturing middle class; division of labor between the different corporate guilds vanished in the face of division of labor in each single workshop.

Meantime the markets kept ever growing, the demand ever rising. Even manufacture no longer sufficed. Thereupon, steam and machinery revolutionized industrial production. The place of manufacture was taken by the giant, Modern Industry, the place of the industrial middle class by industrial millionaires—the leaders of whole industrial armies, the modern bourgeois.

Modern industry has established the world market, for which the discovery of America paved the way. This market has given an immense development to commerce, to navigation, to communication by land. This development has, in its turn, reacted on the extension of industry; and in proportion as industry, commerce, navigation, railways extended, in the same proportion the bourgeoisie developed, increased its capital, and pushed into the background every class handed down from the Middle Ages.

We see, therefore, how the modern bourgeoisie is itself the product of a long course of development, of a series of revolutions in the modes of production and of exchange.

Each step in the development of the bourgeoisie was accompanied by a corresponding political advance of that class. An oppressed class under the sway of the feudal nobility, an armed and self-governing association in the medieval commune;* here independent urban republic (as in Italy and Germany), there taxable "third estate" of the monarchy (as in France), afterward, in the period of manufacture proper, serving either the semi-feudal or the absolute monarchy as a counterpoise against the nobility, and, in fact, cornerstone of the great monarchies in general, the bourgeoisie has at last, since the establishment of Modern Industry and of the world market, conquered for itself, in the modern representative State, exclusive political sway. The executive of the modern State is but a committee for managing the common affairs of the whole bourgeoisie.

The bourgeoisie, historically, has played a most revolutionary part.

The bourgeoisie, wherever it has got the upper hand, has put an end to all feudal, patriarchal, idyllic relations. It has pitilessly torn asunder the motley feudal ties that bound man to his "natural superiors," and has left remaining no other nexus between man and man than naked self-interest, than callous "cash pay-

---

* "Commune" was the name taken in France by the nascent towns even before they had conquered from their feudal lords and masters local self-government and political rights as the "Third Estate." Generally speaking, for the economic development of the bourgeoisie, England is here taken as the typical country; for its political development, France. [*1888*]

This was the name given their urban communities by the townsmen of Italy and France, after they had purchased or wrested their initial rights of self-government from their feudal lords. [*1890*]

ment." It has drowned the most heavenly ecstasies of religious fervor, of chivalrous enthusiasm, of philistine sentimentalism, in the icy water of egotistical calculation. It has resolved personal worth into exchange value, and in place of the numberless indefeasible chartered freedoms has set up that single, unconscionable freedom—Free Trade. In one word, for exploitation, veiled by religious and political illusions, it has substituted naked, shameless, direct, brutal exploitation.

The bourgeoisie has stripped of its halo every occupation hitherto honored and looked up to with reverent awe. It has converted the physician, the lawyer, the priest, the poet, the man of science, into its paid wage-laborers.

The bourgeoisie has torn away from the family its sentimental veil, and has reduced the family relation to a mere money relation.

The bourgeoisie has disclosed how it came to pass that the brutal display of vigor in the Middle Ages, which Reactionists so much admire, found its fitting complement in the most slothful indolence. It has been the first to show what man's activity can bring about. It has accomplished wonders far surpassing Egyptian pyramids, Roman aqueducts and Gothic cathedrals; it has conducted expeditions that put in the shade all former Exoduses of nations and crusades.

The bourgeoisie cannot exist without constantly revolutionizing the instruments of production, and thereby the relations of production, and with them the whole relations of society. Conservation of the old modes of production in unaltered form was, on the contrary, the first condition of existence for all earlier industrial classes. Constant revolutionizing of production, uninterrupted disturbance of all social conditions, everlasting uncertainty and agitation distinguish the bourgeois epoch from all earlier ones. All fixed, fast-frozen relations, with their train of ancient and venerable prejudices and opinions, are swept away, all new-formed ones become antiquated before they can ossify. All that is solid melts into air, all that is holy is profaned, and man is at last compelled to face with sober senses his real conditions of life and his relations with his kind.

The need of a constantly expanding market for its products chases the bourgeoisie over the whole surface of the globe. It must nestle everywhere, settle everywhere, establish connections everywhere.

The bourgeoisie has through its exploitation of the world market given a cosmopolitan character to production and consumption in every country. To the great chagrin of Reactionists, it has drawn from under the feet of industry the national ground on which it stood. All old-established national industries have been destroyed or are daily being destroyed. They are dislodged by new industries, whose introduction becomes a life and death question for all civilized nations, by industries that no longer work up indigenous raw material but raw material drawn from the remotest zones; industries whose products are consumed, not only at home, but in every quarter of the globe. In place of the old wants, satisfied by the production of the country, we find new wants, requiring for their satisfaction the products of distant lands and climes. In place of the old local and national seclusion and self-sufficiency, we have intercourse in every direction, universal interdependence of nations. And as in material, so also in intellectual production. The intellectual creations of individual nations become common property. National one-sidedness and narrow-mindedness become more and more impossible, and from the numerous national and local literatures there arises a world literature.

The bourgeoisie, by the rapid improvement of all instruments of production, by the immensely facilitated means of communication, draws all, even the most barbarian, nations into civilization. The cheap prices of its commodities are the heavy artillery with which it batters down all Chinese walls, with which it forces the barbarians' intensely obstinate hatred of foreigners to capitulate. It compels all nations, on pain of extinction, to adopt the bourgeois mode of production; it compels them to introduce what it calls civilization into their midst, i.e., to become bourgeois themselves. In a word, it creates a world after its own image.

The bourgeoisie has subjected the country to the rule of the towns. It has created enormous cities, has greatly increased the urban population as compared with the rural, and has thus rescued a considerable part of the population from the idiocy of rural life. Just as it has made the country dependent on the towns, so it has made barbarian and semi-barbarian countries dependent on the civilized ones, nations of peasants on nations of bourgeois, the East on the West.

The bourgeoisie keeps doing away more and more with the scattered state of the population, of the means of production, and of property. It has agglomerated population, centralized means of production, and has concentrated property in a few hands. The necessary consequence of this was political centralization. Independent or but loosely connected provinces with separate interests, laws, governments and systems of taxation became lumped together into one nation, with one government, one code of laws, one national class interest, one frontier and one customs tariff.

The bourgeoisie during its rule of scarce one hundred years has created more massive and more colossal productive forces than have all preceding generations together. Subjection of nature's forces to man, machinery, application of chemistry to industry and agriculture, steam navigation, railways, electric telegraphs, clearing of whole continents for cultivation, canalization of rivers, whole populations conjured out of the ground—what earlier century had even a presentiment that such productive forces slumbered in the lap of social labor?

We see then: the means of production and of exchange, on the foundation of which the bourgeoisie built itself up, were generated in feudal society. At a certain stage in the development of these means of production and of exchange, the conditions under which feudal society produced and exchanged, the feudal organization of agriculture and manufacturing industry, in a word, the feudal relations of property became no longer compatible with the already developed productive forces; they became so many fetters. They had to be burst asunder; they were burst asunder.

Into their place stepped free competition, accompanied by a social and political constitution adapted to it and by the economic and political sway of the bourgeois class.

A similar movement is going on before our own eyes. Modern bourgeois society with its relations of production, of exchange and of property, a society that has conjured up such gigantic means of production and of exchange, is like the sorcerer who is no longer able to control the powers of the nether world whom he has called up by his spells. For many a decade past the history of industry and commerce is but the history of the revolt of modern productive forces against modern conditions of production, against the property relations that are the conditions for the existence of the bourgeoisie and of its rule. It is enough to mention the commercial crises that by their periodical return put on trial, each time more threateningly, the existence of the entire bourgeois society. In these crises a great part not only of the existing products, but also of the previously created productive forces, are periodically destroyed. In these crises there breaks out an epidemic that in all earlier epochs would have seemed an absurdity —the epidemic of over-production. Society suddenly finds itself put back into a state of momentary barbarism; it appears as if a famine, a universal war of devastation had cut off the supply of every means of subsistence; industry and commerce seem to be destroyed; and why? Because there is too much civilization, too much means of subsistence, too much industry, too much commerce. The productive forces at the disposal of society no longer tend to further the development of the conditions of bourgeois property; on the contrary, they have become too powerful for these conditions, by which they are fettered, and as soon as they overcome these fetters, they bring disorder into the whole of bourgeois society, endanger the existence of bourgeois property. The conditions of bourgeois society are too narrow to comprise the wealth created by them. And how does the bourgeoisie get over these crises? On the one hand by enforced destruction of a mass of productive forces; on the other, by the conquest of new markets and by the more thorough exploitation of the old ones. That is to say, by paving the way for more extensive and more destructive crises and by diminishing the means whereby crises are prevented.

The weapons with which the bourgeoisie felled feudalism to the ground are now turned against the bourgeoisie itself.

But not only has the bourgeoisie forged the weapons that bring death to itself; it has also called into existence the men who are to wield those weapons—the modern working class, the proletarians.

In proportion as the bourgeoisie, i.e., capital, is developed, in the same proportion is the proletariat, the modern working class, developed—a class of laborers who live only as long as they find work, and who find work only as long as their labor increases capital. These laborers, who must sell themselves piecemeal, are a commodity like every other article of commerce, and are consequently exposed to all the vicissitudes of competition, to all the fluctuations of the market.

Owing to the extensive use of machinery and to division of labor, the work of the proletarians has lost all individual character and, consequently, all charm for the workman. He becomes an appendage of the machine, and it is only the most simple, most monotonous, and most easily acquired knack that is required of him. Hence, the cost of production of a workman is restricted almost entirely to the means of subsistence that he requires for his maintenance and for the propagation of his race. But the price of a commodity, and therefore also of labor,[2] is equal to its cost of production. In proportion, therefore, as the repulsiveness of the work increases, the wage decreases. Nay more, in proportion as the use of machinery and division of labor increase, in the same proportion the burden of toil also increases, whether by prolongation of the working hours, by increase of the work exacted in a given time or by increased speed of the machinery, etc.

Modern industry has converted the little workshop of the patriarchal master into the great factory of the industrial capitalist. Masses of laborers, crowded into the factory, are organized like soldiers. As privates of the industrial army they are placed under the command of a perfect hierarchy of officers and sergeants. Not only are they slaves of the bourgeois class and of the bourgeois State; they are daily and hourly enslaved by the machine, by the overseer and, above all, by the individual bourgeois manufacturer himself. The more openly this despotism proclaims gain to be its end and aim, the more petty, the more hateful and the more embittering it is.

The less the skill and exertion of strength implied in manual labor, in other words, the more modern industry becomes developed, the more is the labor of men superseded by that of women. Differences of age and sex no longer have any distinctive social validity for the working class. All are instruments of labor, more or less expensive to use, according to their age and sex.

No sooner is the exploitation of the laborer by the manufacturer so far at an end that he receives his wages in cash, than he is set upon by the other portions of the bourgeoisie, the landlord, the shopkeeper, the pawnbroker, etc.

The lower strata of the middle class—the small tradespeople, shopkeepers and retired tradesmen generally, the handicraftsmen and peasants—all these sink gradually into the proletariat, partly because their diminutive capital does not suffice for the scale on which Modern Industry is carried on and is swamped in the competition with the large capitalists, partly because their specialized skill is rendered worthless by new methods of production. Thus the proletariat is recruited from all classes of the population.

The proletariat goes through various stages of development. With its birth begins its struggle with the bourgeoisie. At first the contest is carried on by individual laborers, then by the work people of a factory, then by the operatives of one trade in one locality against the individual bourgeois who directly exploits them. They direct their attacks not against the bourgeois conditions of production, but against the instruments of production themselves; they destroy imported wares that compete with their labor, they smash machinery to pieces, they set factories ablaze, they seek to restore by force the vanished status of the workman of the Middle Ages.

At this stage the laborers still form an incoherent mass scattered over the whole country and broken up by their mutual competition. If anywhere they unite to form more compact bodies, this is not yet the consequence of their own active union but of the union of the bourgeoisie, which class, in order to attain its own political ends, is compelled to set the whole proletariat in motion and, moreover is, for a time, yet able to do so. At this stage, therefore, the proletarians do not fight their enemies, but the enemies of their enemies, the remnants of absolute monarchy, the landowners, the non-industrial bourgeois, the petty bourgeoisie. Thus the whole historical movement is concentrated in the hands of the bourgeoisie; every victory so obtained is a victory for the bourgeoisie.

But with the development of industry the proletariat not only increases in number; it becomes concentrated in greater masses, its strength grows, and it feels that strength more. The various interests and conditions of life within the ranks of the proletariat are more and more equalized in proportion as machinery obliterates all distinctions of labor and nearly everywhere reduces wages to the same low level. The growing competition among the bourgeois, and the resulting commercial crises, make the wages of the workers ever more fluctuating. The unceasing improvement of machinery, ever more rapidly developing, makes their livelihood more and more precarious; the collisions between individual workmen and individual bourgeois take more and more the character of collisions between two classes. Thereupon the workers begin to form combinations (Trades' Unions) against the bourgeois; they club together in order to keep up the rate of wages; they found permanent associations in order to make provision beforehand for these occasional revolts. Here and there the contest breaks out into riots.

Now and then the workers are victorious, but only for a time. The real fruit of their battles lies, not in the immediate result, but in the ever expanding union of the workers. This union is helped on by the improved means of communication that are created by modern industry and that place the workers of different localities in contact with one another. It was just this contact that was needed to centralize the numerous local struggles, all of the same character, into one national struggle between classes. But every class struggle is a political struggle. And that union, to attain which the burghers of the Middle Ages with their misera-

ble highways required centuries, the modern proletarians, thanks
to railways, achieve in a few years.

This organization of the proletarians into a class and consequently into a political party is continually being upset again by
the competition between the workers themselves. But it ever
rises up again, stronger, firmer, mightier. It compels legislative
recognition of particular interests of the workers, by taking advantage of the divisions among the bourgeoisie itself. Thus the
ten-hours' bill in England was carried.

Altogether, collisions between the classes of the old society in
many ways further the course of development of the proletariat.
The bourgeoisie finds itself involved in a constant battle. At first
with the aristocracy; later on, with those portions of the bourgeoisie itself whose interests have become antagonistic to the progress of industry; at all times with the bourgeoisie of foreign
countries. In all these battles it sees itself compelled to appeal to
the proletariat, to ask for its help, and thus to drag it into the political arena. The bourgeoisie itself, therefore, supplies the proletariat with its own elements of political and general education; in
other words, it furnishes the proletariat with weapons for fighting
the bourgeoisie.

Further, as we have already seen, entire sections of the ruling
classes are precipitated into the proletariat by the advance of industry, or are at least threatened in their conditions of existence.
These also supply the proletariat with fresh elements of enlightenment and progress.

Finally, in times when the class struggle nears the decisive
hour, the process of dissolution going on within the ruling class,
in fact within the whole range of old society, assumes such a violent, glaring character that a small section of the ruling class cuts
itself adrift and joins the revolutionary class, the class that holds
the future in its hands. Therefore, just as, at an earlier period a
section of the nobility went over to the bourgeoisie, so now a
portion of the bourgeoisie goes over to the proletariat, and in
particular a portion of the bourgeois ideologists who have raised
themselves to the level of comprehending theoretically the historical movement as a whole.

Of all the classes that stand face to face with the bourgeoisie today, the proletariat alone is a really revolutionary class. The other classes decay and finally disappear in the face of modern industry; the proletariat is its special and essential product.

The lower middle class, the small manufacturer, the shopkeeper, the artisan, the peasant, all these fight against the bourgeoisie to save from extinction their existence as fractions of the middle class. They are therefore not revolutionary, but conservative. Nay more, they are reactionary, for they try to roll back the wheel of history. If by chance they are revolutionary, they are so only in view of their impending transfer into the proletariat; they thus defend not their present, but their future interests; they desert their own standpoint to place themselves at that of the proletariat.

The "dangerous class," the social scum, that passively rotting mass thrown off by the lowest layers of the old society may here and there be swept into the movement by a proletarian revolution; its conditions of life, however, prepare it far more for the part of a bribed tool of reactionary intrigue.

In the conditions of the proletariat, those of the old society at large are already virtually swamped. The proletarian is without property; his relation to his wife and children has no longer anything in common with the bourgeois family relations; modern industrial labor, modern subjection to capital, the same in England as in France, in America as in Germany, has stripped him of every trace of national character. Law, morality, religion are to him so many bourgeois prejudices behind which lurk in ambush just as many bourgeois interests.   .

All the preceding classes that got the upper hand sought to fortify their already acquired status by subjecting society at large to their conditions of appropriation. The proletarians cannot become masters of the productive forces of society except by abolishing their own previous mode of appropriation, and thereby also every other previous mode of appropriation. They have nothing of their own to secure and to fortify; their mission is to destroy all previous securities for, and insurances of, individual property.

All previous historical movements were movements of minorities or in the interest of minorities. The proletarian movement is the self-conscious, independent movement of the immense majority in the interest of the immense majority. The proletariat, the lowest stratum of our present society, cannot stir, cannot raise itself up, without the whole superincumbent strata of official society being sprung into the air.

Though not in substance, yet in form, the struggle of the proletariat with the bourgeoisie is at first a national struggle. The proletariat of each country must, of course, first of all settle matters with its own bourgeoisie.

In depicting the most general phases of the development of the proletariat, we traced the more or less veiled civil war raging within existing society up to the point where that war breaks out into open revolution, and where the violent overthrow of the bourgeoisie lays the foundation for the sway of the proletariat.

Hitherto, every form of society has been based, as we have already seen, on the antagonism of oppressing and oppressed classes. But in order to oppress a class certain conditions must be assured to it under which it can, at least, continue its slavish existence. The serf, in the period of serfdom, raised himself to membership in the commune, just as the petty bourgeois, under the yoke of feudal absolutism, managed to develop into a bourgeois. The modern laborer, on the contrary, instead of rising with the progress of industry sinks deeper and deeper below the conditions of existence of his own class. He becomes a pauper, and pauperism develops more rapidly than population and wealth. And here it becomes evident that the bourgeoisie is unfit any longer to be the ruling class in society and to impose its conditions of existence upon society as an over-riding law. It is unfit to rule because it is incompetent to assure an existence to its slave within his slavery, because it cannot help letting him sink into such a state that it has to feed him instead of being fed by him. Society can no longer live under this bourgeoisie, in other words, its existence is no longer compatible with society.

The essential condition for the existence and for the sway of the bourgeois class is the formation and augmentation of capital; the condition for capital is wage labor. Wage labor rests exclusively on competition between the laborers. The advance of industry, whose involuntary promoter is the bourgeoisie, replaces the isolation of the laborers, due to competition, by their revolutionary combination due to association. The development of Modern Industry therefore cuts from under its feet the very foundation on which the bourgeoisie produces and appropriates products. What the bourgeoisie therefore produces, above all, are its own grave-diggers. Its fall and the victory of the proletariat are equally inevitable.

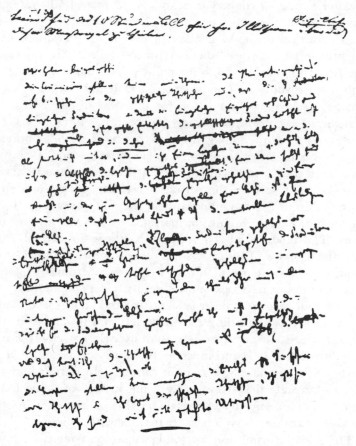

The only page preserved from the original manuscript of the *Communist Manifesto*. The text is in Marx's hand, except for the first two lines which were dictated by him and written by his wife, Jenny.

II. PROLETARIANS AND COMMUNISTS

In what relation do the Communists stand to the proletarians as a whole?

The Communists do not form a separate party opposed to other working-class parties.

They have no interests separate and apart from those of the proletariat as a whole.

They do not set up any sectarian principles of their own by which to shape and mold the proletarian movement.

The Communists are distinguished from the other working-class parties by this only: (1) In the national struggles of the proletarians of the different countries they point out and bring to the front the common interests of the entire proletariat, independently of all nationality. (2) In the various stages of development which the struggle of the working class against the bourgeoisie has to pass through, they always and everywhere represent the interests of the movement as a whole.

The Communists therefore are on the one hand, practically, the most advanced and resolute section of the working-class parties of every country, that section which pushes forward all others; on the other hand, theoretically, they have over the great mass of the proletariat the advantage of clearly understanding the line of march, the conditions, and the ultimate general results of the proletarian movement.

The immediate aim of the Communists is the same as that of all the other proletarian parties: formation of the proletariat into a class, overthrow of the bourgeois supremacy, conquest of political power by the proletariat.

The theoretical conclusions of the Communists are in no way based on ideas or principles that have been invented or discovered by this or that would-be universal reformer.

They merely express, in general terms, actual relations springing from an existing class struggle, from a historical movement going on under our very eyes. The abolition of existing property relations is not at all a distinctive feature of Communism.

All property relations in the past have continually been subject to historical change consequent upon the change in historical conditions.

The French Revolution, for example, abolished feudal property in favor of bourgeois property.

The distinguishing feature of Communism is not the abolition of property generally, but the abolition of bourgeois property. But modern bourgeois private property is the final and most complete expression of the system of producing and appropriating products, that is based on class antagonisms, on the exploitation of the many by the few.

In this sense, the theory of the Communists may be summed up in the single sentence: Abolition of private property.

We Communists have been reproached with the desire of abolishing the right of personally acquiring property as the fruit of a man's own labor, which property is alleged to be the groundwork of all personal freedom, activity and independence.

Hard-won, self-acquired, self-earned property! Do you mean the property of the petty artisan and of the small peasant, a form of property that preceded the bourgeois form? There is no need to abolish that; the development of industry has to a great extent already destroyed it, and is still destroying it daily.

Or do you mean modern bourgeois private property?

But does wage labor create any property for the laborer? Not a bit. It creates capital, i.e., that kind of property which exploits wage labor and which cannot increase except upon condition of begetting a new supply of wage labor for fresh exploitation. Property, in its present form, is based on the antagonism of capital and wage labor. Let us examine both sides of this antagonism.

To be a capitalist, is to have not only a purely personal but a social *status* in production. Capital is a collective product, and only by the united action of many members, nay, in the last resort, only by the united action of all members of society, can it be set in motion.

Capital is, therefore, not a personal, it is a social power.

When therefore capital is converted into common property, into the property of all members of society, personal property is not thereby transformed into social property. It is only the social character of the property that is changed. It loses its class character.

Let us now take wage labor.

The average price of wage labor is the minimum wage, i.e., that quantum of the means of subsistence which is absolutely requisite to keep the laborer in bare existence as a laborer. What, therefore, the wage-laborer appropriates by means of his labor merely suffices to prolong and reproduce a bare existence. We by no means intend to abolish this personal appropriation of the products of labor, an appropriation that is made for the maintenance and reproduction of human life and that leaves no surplus wherewith to command the labor of others. All that we want to do away with is the miserable character of this appropriation, under which the laborer lives merely to increase capital and is allowed to live only in so far as the interest of the ruling class requires it.

In bourgeois society, living labor is but a means to increase accumulated labor. In Communist society, accumulated labor is but a means to widen, to enrich, to promote the existence of the laborer.

In bourgeois society, therefore, the past dominates the present; in Communist society the present dominates the past. In bourgeois society capital is independent and has individuality, while the living person is dependent and has no individuality.

And the abolition of this state of things is called by the bourgeois abolition of individuality and freedom! And rightly so. The abolition of bourgeois individuality, bourgeois independence and bourgeois freedom is undoubtedly aimed at.

By freedom is meant, under the present bourgeois conditions of production, free trade, free selling and buying.

But if selling and buying disappears, free selling and buying disappears also. This talk about free selling and buying and all the other "brave words" of our bourgeoisie about freedom in general have a meaning, if any, only in contrast with restricted selling and buying, with the fettered traders of the Middle Ages, but have no meaning when opposed to the Communist abolition of buying and selling, of the bourgeois conditions of production, and of the bourgeoisie itself.

You are horrified at our intending to do away with private property. But in your existing society private property is already done away with for nine-tenths of the population; its existence for the few is solely due to its non-existence in the hands of those nine-tenths. You reproach us, therefore, with intending to do away with a form of property, the necessary condition for whose existence is the non-existence of any property for the immense majority of society.

In a word, you reproach us with intending to do away with your property. Precisely so; that is just what we intend.

From the moment when labor can no longer be converted into capital, money, or rent, into a social power capable of being monopolized, i.e., from the moment when individual property can no longer be transformed into bourgeois property, into capital, from that moment, you say, individuality vanishes.

You must, therefore, confess that by "individual" you mean no other person than the bourgeois, than the middle-class owner of property. This person must, indeed, be swept out of the way and made impossible.

Communism deprives no man of the power to appropriate the products of society; all that it does is to deprive him of the power to subjugate the labor of others by means of such appropriation.

It has been objected that upon the abolition of private property all work will cease and universal laziness will overtake us.

According to this, bourgeois society ought long ago to have gone to the dogs through sheer idleness; for those of its members who work acquire nothing, and those who acquire anything do not work. The whole of this objection is but another expression of the tautology: there can no longer be any wage labor when there is no longer any capital.

All objections urged against the Communistic mode of producing and appropriating material products have in the same way been urged against the Communistic modes of producing and appropriating intellectual products. Just as, to the bourgeois, the disappearance of class property is the disappearance of production itself, so the disappearance of class culture is to him identical with the disappearance of all culture.

That culture, the loss of which he laments, is for the enormous majority a mere training to act as a machine.

But don't wrangle with us so long as you apply to our intended abolition of bourgeois property the standard of your bourgeois notions of freedom, culture, law, etc. Your very ideas are but the outgrowth of the conditions of your bourgeois production and bourgeois property, just as your jurisprudence is but the will of your class made into a law for all, a will whose essential character and direction are determined by the economic conditions of existence of your class.

The selfish misconception that induces you to transform into eternal laws of nature and of reason the social forms springing from your present mode of production and form of property—historical relations that rise and disappear in the progress of production—this misconception you share with every ruling class that has preceded you. What you see clearly in the case of ancient property, what you admit in the case of feudal property, you are of course forbidden to admit in the case of your own bourgeois form of property.

Abolition of the family! Even the most radical flare up at this infamous proposal of the Communists.

On what foundation is the present family, the bourgeois family, based? On capital, on private gain. In its completely developed form this family exists only among the bourgeoisie. But this state of things finds its complement in the practical absence of the family among the proletarians, and in public prostitution.

The bourgeois family will vanish as a matter of course when its complement vanishes, and both will vanish with the vanishing of capital.

Do you charge us with wanting to stop the exploitation of children by their parents? To this crime we plead guilty.

But, you will say, we destroy the most hallowed of relations when we replace home education by social.

And your education! Is not that also social, and determined by the social conditions under which you educate, by the intervention, direct or indirect, of society, by means of schools, etc.? The Communists have not invented the intervention of society in education; they do but seek to alter the character of that intervention, and to rescue education from the influence of the ruling class.

The bourgeois claptrap about the family and education, about the hallowed correlation of parent and child, becomes all the more disgusting the more, by the action of Modern Industry, all family ties among the proletarians are torn asunder and their children transformed into simple articles of commerce and instruments of labor.

But you Communists would introduce community of women, screams the whole bourgeoisie in chorus.

The bourgeois sees in his wife a mere instrument of production. He hears that the instruments of production are to be exploited in common, and, naturally, can come to no other conclusion than that the lot of being common to all will likewise fall to the women.

He has not even a suspicion that the real point aimed at is to do away with the status of women as mere instruments of production.

For the rest, nothing is more ridiculous than the virtuous indignation of our bourgeois at the community of women which, they pretend, is to be openly and officially established by the Communists. The Communists have no need to introduce community of women; it has existed almost from time immemorial.

Our bourgeois, not content with having the wives and daughters of their proletarians at their disposal, not to speak of common prostitutes, take the greatest pleasure in seducing each other's wives.

Bourgeois marriage is in reality a system of wives in common and thus, at the most, what the Communists might possibly be reproached with is that they desire to introduce, in substitution for a hypocritically concealed, an openly legalized community of women. For the rest, it is self-evident that the abolition of the present system of production must bring with it the abolition of the community of women springing from that system, i.e., of prostitution both public and private.

The Communists are further reproached with desiring to abolish countries and nationality.

The workingmen have no country. We cannot take from them what they have not got. Since the proletariat must first of all acquire political supremacy, must rise to be the leading class of the nation, must constitute itself as the nation, it is so far itself national, though not in·the bourgeois sense of the word.

National differences and antagonisms between peoples are vanishing daily more and more owing to the development of the bourgeoisie, to freedom of commerce, to the world market, to uniformity in the mode of production and in the conditions of life corresponding thereto.

The supremacy of the proletariat will cause them to vanish still faster. United action, of the leading civilized countries at least, is one of the first conditions for the emancipation of the proletariat.

In proportion as the exploitation of one individual by another is put to an end, the exploitation of one nation by another will also be put to an end. In proportion as the antagonism between classes within the nation vanishes, the hostility of one nation to another will come to an end.

The charges against Communism made from a religious, a philosophical and generally from an ideological standpoint, are not deserving of serious examination.

Does it require deep intuition to comprehend that man's ideas, views and conceptions, in one word, man's consciousness, changes with every change in the conditions of his material existence, in his social relations and in his social life?

What else does the history of ideas prove than that intellectual production changes its character in proportion as material production is changed? The ruling ideas of each age have ever been the ideas of its ruling class.

When people speak of ideas that revolutionize society they do but express the fact that within the old society the elements of a new one have been created, and that the dissolution of the old ideas keeps even pace with the dissolution of the old conditions of existence.

When the ancient world was in its last throes the ancient religions were overcome by Christianity. When Christian ideas succumbed in the 18th century to rationalist ideas, feudal society fought its death battle with the then revolutionary bourgeoisie. The ideas of religious liberty and freedom of conscience merely gave expression to the sway of free competition within the domain of knowledge.

"Undoubtedly," it will be said, "religious, moral, philosophical and juridical ideas have been modified in the course of historical development. But religion, morality, philosophy, political science, and law, constantly survived this change.

"There are, besides, eternal truths, such as Freedom, Justice, etc., that are common to all states of society. But Communism abolishes eternal truths, it abolishes all religion and all morality, instead of constituting them on a new basis; it therefore acts in contradiction to all past historical experience."

What does this accusation reduce itself to? The history of all past society has consisted in the development of class antagonisms, antagonisms that assumed different forms at different epochs.

But whatever form they may have taken, one fact is common to all past ages, viz., the exploitation of one part of society by the other. No wonder, then, that the social consciousness of past ages, despite all the multiplicity and variety it displays, moves within certain common forms, or general ideas, which cannot completely vanish except with the total disappearance of class antagonisms.

The Communist revolution is the most radical rupture with traditional property relations; no wonder that its development involves the most radical rupture with traditional ideas.

But let us have done with the bourgeois objections to Communism.

We have seen above that the first step in the revolution by the working class is to raise the proletariat to the position of ruling class, to win the battle of democracy.

The proletariat will use its political supremacy to wrest, by degrees, all capital from the bourgeoisie, to centralize all instruments of production in the hands of the State, i.e., of the proletariat organized as the ruling class; and to increase the total of productive forces as rapidly as possible.

Of course, in the beginning this cannot be effected except by means of despotic inroads on the rights of property and on the conditions of bourgeois production; by means of measures, therefore, which appear economically insufficient and untenable but which, in the course of the movement, outstrip themselves, necessitate further inroads upon the old social order, and are unavoidable as a means of entirely revolutionizing the mode of production.

These measures will of course be different in different countries.[1]

Nevertheless in the most advanced countries, the following will be pretty generally applicable:

1. Abolition of property in land and application of all rents of land to public purposes.[2]

2. A heavy progressive or graduated income tax.[3]

3. Abolition of all right of inheritance.[4]

4. Confiscation of the property of all emigrants and rebels.[5]

5. Centralization of credit in the hands of the State, by means of a national bank with State capital and an exclusive monopoly.[6]

6. Centralization of the means of communication and transport in the hands of the State.

7. Extension of factories and instruments of production owned by the State; the bringing into cultivation of wastelands, and the improvement of the soil generally in accordance with a common plan.

8. Equal liability of all to labor. Establishment of industrial armies, especially for agriculture.[7]

9. Combination of agriculture with manufacturing industries;

gradual abolition of the distinction between town and country by a more equable distribution of the population over the country.[8]

10. Free education for all children in public schools. Abolition of children's factory labor in its present form. Combination of education with industrial production, etc., etc.[9]

When in the course of development class distinctions have disappeared and all production has been concentrated in the hands of a vast association of the whole nation, the public power will lose its political character. Political power, properly so called, is merely the organized power of one class for oppressing another. If the proletariat during its contest with the bourgeoisie is compelled, by the force of circumstances, to organize itself as a class, if by means of a revolution it makes itself the ruling class and, as such, sweeps away by force the old conditions of production, then it will, along with these conditions, have swept away the conditions for the existence of class antagonisms and of classes generally, and will thereby have abolished its own supremacy as a class.

In place of the old bourgeois society, with its classes and class antagonisms, we shall have an association in which the free development of each is the condition for the free development of all.

III. SOCIALIST AND COMMUNIST LITERATURE

1. REACTIONARY SOCIALISM

a. Feudal Socialism

Owing to their historical position, it became the vocation of the aristocracies of France and England to write pamphlets against modern bourgeois society. In the French revolution of July 1830 and in English reform agitation these aristocracies again succumbed to the hateful upstart. Thenceforth, a serious political contest was altogether out of question. A literary battle alone remained possible. But even in the domain of literature the old cries of the restoration period* had become impossible.

In order to arouse sympathy, apparently the aristocracy were obliged to lose sight of their own interests, and to formulate their indictment against the bourgeoisie in the interest of the exploited working class alone. Thus the aristocracy took their revenge by singing lampoons on their new master and whispering in his ears sinister prophecies of coming catastrophe.

In this way arose Feudal Socialism: half lamentation, half lampoon; half echo of the past, half menace of the future; at times, by its bitter, witty and incisive criticism, striking the bourgeoisie to the very heart's core; but always ludicrous in its effect through total incapacity to comprehend the march of modern history.

The aristocracy, in order to rally the people to them, waved the proletarian alms-bag in front for a banner. But the people, so

* Not the English Restoration, 1660 to 1689, but the French Restoration, 1814 to 1830. [*1888*]

often as it joined them, saw on their hindquarters the old feudal coats of arms and deserted with loud and irreverent laughter. One section of the French Legitimists[1] and "Young England"[2] exhibited this spectacle.

In pointing out that their mode of exploitation was different than that of the bourgeoisie, the feudalists forget that they exploited under circumstances and conditions that were quite different and that are now antiquated. In showing that under their rule the modern proletariat never existed, they forget that the modern bourgeoisie is the necessary offspring of their own form of society.

For the rest, so little do they conceal the reactionary character of their criticism that their chief accusation against the bourgeoisie amounts to this, that under the bourgeois *régime* a class is being developed which is destined to cut up root and branch the old order of society.

What they upbraid the bourgeoisie with is not so much that it creates a proletariat as that it creates a *revolutionary* proletariat.

In political practice, therefore, they join in all coercive measures against the working class; and in ordinary life, despite their high-falutin phrases, they stoop to pick up the golden apples dropped from the tree of industry and to barter truth, love, and honor for traffic in wool, beetroot-sugar and potato spirits.*

As the parson has ever gone hand in hand with the landlord, so has Clerical Socialism with Feudal Socialism.[3]

Nothing is easier than to give Christian asceticism a Socialist tinge. Has not Christianity declaimed against private property, against marriage, against the State? Has it not preached in the place of these, charity and poverty, celibacy and mortification of the flesh, monastic life and Mother Church? Christian Socialism is but the holy water with which the priest consecrates the heart-burnings of the aristocrat.

---

*This applies chiefly to Germany where the landed aristocracy and squirearchy have large portions of their estates cultivated for their own account by stewards, and are, moreover, extensively beetroot-sugar manufacturers and distillers of potato spirits. The wealthier British aristocracy are, as yet, rather above that; but they, too, know how to make up for declining rents by lending their names to floaters of more or less shady joint-stock companies. [*1888*]

b. Petty-Bourgeois Socialism

The feudal aristocracy was not the only class that was ruined by the bourgeoisie, not the only class whose conditions of existence pined and perished in the atmosphere of modern bourgeois society. The medieval burgesses and the small peasant proprietors were the precursors of the modern bourgeoisie. In those countries which are but little developed, industrially and commercially, these two classes still vegetate side by side with the rising bourgeoisie.

In countries where modern civilization has become fully developed a new class of petty bourgeois has been formed, fluctuating between proletariat and bourgeoisie and ever renewing itself as a supplementary part of bourgeois society. The individual members of this class, however, are being constantly hurled down into the proletariat by the action of competition, and as modern industry develops they even see the moment approaching when they will disappear completely as an independent section of modern society, to be replaced in manufactures, agriculture and commerce by overseers, bailiffs and shopmen.

In countries like France, where the peasants constitute far more than half of the population, it was natural that writers who sided with the proletariat against the bourgeoisie, should use in their criticism of the bourgeois *régime* the standard of the peasant and petty bourgeois, and from the standpoint of these intermediate classes should take up the cudgels for the working class. Thus arose petty-bourgeois Socialism. Sismondi was the head of this school, not only in France but also in England.[4]

This school of Socialism dissected with great acuteness the contradictions in the conditions of modern production. It laid bare the hypocritical apologies of economists. It proved, incontrovertibly, the disastrous effects of machinery and division of labor, the concentration of capital and land in a few hands, over-production and crises; it pointed out the inevitable ruin of the petty bourgeois and peasant, the misery of the proletariat, the anarchy in production, the crying inequalities in the distribution of wealth, the industrial war of extermination between nations, the dissolution of old moral bonds, of the old family relations, of the old nationalities.

In its positive aims, however, this form of Socialism aspires either to restoring the old means of production and of exchange, and with them the old property relations and the old society, or to cramping the modern means of production and of exchange within the framework of the old property relations that have been, and were bound to be, exploded by those means. In either case, it is both reactionary and Utopian.

Its last words are: corporate guilds for manufacture; patriarchal relations in agriculture.

Ultimately, when stubborn historical facts had dispersed all intoxicating effects of self-deception, this form of Socialism ended in a miserable fit of the blues.

c. German or "True" Socialism

The Socialist and Communist literature of France, a literature that originated under the pressure of a bourgeoisie in power and that was the expression of the struggle against this power, was introduced into Germany at a time when the bourgeoisie in that country had just begun its contest with feudal absolutism.

German philosophers, would-be philosophers, and *beaux esprits* eagerly seized on this literature, only forgetting that when these writings immigrated from France into Germany, French social conditions had not immigrated along with them. In contact with German social conditions, this French literature lost all its immediate practical significance and assumed a purely literary aspect. Thus, to the German philosophers of the 18th century, the demands of the first French Revolution were nothing more than the demands of "Practical Reason"[5] in general, and the utterance of the will of the revolutionary French bourgeoisie signified in their eyes the laws of pure Will, of Will as it was bound to be, of true human Will generally.

The work of the German *literati* consisted solely in bringing the new French ideas into harmony with their ancient philosophical conscience or, rather, in annexing the French ideas without deserting their own philosophic point of view.

This annexation took place in the same way in which a foreign language is appropriated, namely, by translation.

It is well known how the monks wrote silly lives of Catholic Saints *over* the manuscripts on which the classical works of ancient heathendom had been written. The German *literati* reversed this process with the profane French literature. They wrote their philosophical nonsense beneath the French original. For instance, beneath the French criticism of the economic functions of money, they wrote "Alienation of Humanity," and beneath the French criticism of the bourgeois State they wrote, "Dethronement of the Category of the General," and so forth.

The introduction of these philosophical phrases at the back of the French historical criticisms they dubbed "Philosophy of Action," "True Socialism," "German Science of Socialism," "Philosophical Foundation of Socialism," and so on.

The French Socialist and Communist literature was thus completely emasculated. And since it ceased in the hands of the German to express the struggle of one class with the other, he felt conscious of having overcome "French one-sidedness" and of representing, not true requirements, but the requirements of Truth; not the interests of the proletariat, but the interests of Human Nature, of Man in general, who belongs to no class, has no reality, who exists only in the misty realm of philosophical fantasy.

This German Socialism, which took its schoolboy task so seriously and solemnly and extolled its poor stock-in-trade in such mountebank fashion, meanwhile gradually lost its pedantic innocence.

The fight of the German and especially of the Prussian bourgeoisie against feudal aristocracy and absolute monarchy, in other words, the liberal movement, became more earnest.

By this, the long-wished-for opportunity was offered to "True" Socialism of confronting the political movement with the Socialist demands, of hurling the traditional anathemas against liberalism, against representative government, against bourgeois competition, bourgeois freedom of the press, bourgeois legislation, bourgeois liberty and equality, and of preaching to the masses that they had nothing to gain, and everything to lose, by this bourgeois movement. German Socialism forgot in the nick of time that the French criticism, whose silly echo it was, presupposed the existence of modern bourgeois society, with its corresponding economic conditions of existence and the political constitution adapted thereto, the very things whose attainment was the object of the pending struggle in Germany.

To the absolute governments, with their following of parsons, professors, country squires and officials, it served as a welcome scarecrow against the threatening bourgeoisie.

It was a sweet finish after the bitter pills of floggings and bullets with which these same governments, just at that time, dosed the German working-class risings.

While this "True" Socialism thus served the governments as a weapon for fighting the German bourgeoisie, at the same time it directly represented a reactionary interest, the interest of the German Philistines. In Germany the *petty-bourgeois* class, a relic of the 16th century, and since then constantly cropping up again under various forms, is the real social basis of the existing state of things.

To preserve this class is to preserve the existing state of things in Germany. The industrial and political supremacy of the bourgeoisie threatens it with certain destruction—on the one hand, from the concentration of capital; on the other, from the rise of a revolutionary proletariat. "True" Socialism appeared to kill these two birds with one stone. It spread like an epidemic.

The robe of speculative cobwebs, embroidered with flowers of rhetoric, steeped in the dew of sickly sentiment, this transcendental robe in which the German Socialists wrapped their sorry "eternal truths," all skin and bone, served wonderfully to increase the sale of their goods amongst such a public.

And on its part, German Socialism recognized more and more its own calling as the bombastic representative of the petty-bourgeois Philistine.

It proclaimed the German nation to be the model nation and the German petty Philistine to be the typical man. To every villainous meanness of this model man it gave a hidden, higher, Socialistic interpretation, the exact contrary of its real character. It

went to the extreme length of directly opposing the "brutally destructive" tendency of Communism, and of proclaiming its supreme and impartial contempt of all class struggles. With very
few exceptions, all the so-called Socialist and Communist publications that now (1847) circulate in Germany belong to the domain of this foul and enervating literature.*

2. CONSERVATIVE OR BOURGEOIS SOCIALISM

A part of the bourgeoisie is desirous of redressing social grievances in order to secure the continued existence of bourgeois society.

To this section belong economists, philanthropists, humanitarians, improvers of the condition of the working class, organizers
of charity, members of societies for the prevention of cruelty to
animals, temperance fanatics, hole-and-corner reformers of
every imaginable kind. This form of Socialism has, moreover,
been worked out into complete systems.

We may cite Proudhon's *Philosophie de la Misère* as an example of this form.

The Socialistic bourgeois want all the advantages of modern
social conditions without the struggles and dangers necessarily
resulting therefrom. They desire the existing state of society
minus its revolutionary and disintegrating elements. They wish
for a bourgeoisie without a proletariat. The bourgeoisie naturally
conceives the world in which it is supreme to be the best; and
bourgeois Socialism develops this comfortable conception into
various more or less complete systems. In requiring the proletariat to carry out such a system, and thereby to march straightway
into the social New Jerusalem, it but requires in reality that the
proletariat should remain within the bounds of existing society,
but should cast away all its hateful ideas concerning the bourgeoisie.

* The revolutionary storm of 1848 swept away this whole shabby
tendency and cured its protagonists of the desire to dabble further in
Socialism. The chief representative and classical type of this tendency
is Herr Karl Grün. [*1890*]

A second and more practical, but less systematic, form of this Socialism sought to depreciate every revolutionary movement in the eyes of the working class by showing that no mere political reform, but only a change in the material conditions of existence, in economic relations, could be of any advantage to them. By changes in the material conditions of existence this form of Socialism, however, by no means understands abolition of the bourgeois relations of production, an abolition that can be effected only by a revolution, but administrative reforms, based on the continued existence of these relations; reforms, therefore, that in no respect affect the relations between capital and labor, but at the best lessen the cost and simplify the administrative work of bourgeois government.

Bourgeois Socialism attains adequate expression when, and only when, it becomes a mere figure of speech.

Free trade: for the benefit of the working class. Protective duties: for the benefit of the working class. Prison reform: for the benefit of the working class. This is the last word and the only seriously meant word of bourgeois Socialism.

It is summed up in the phrase: the bourgeois is a bourgeois —for the benefit of the working class.

3. CRITICAL-UTOPIAN SOCIALISM AND COMMUNISM

We do not here refer to that literature which in every great modern revolution has always given voice to the demands of the proletariat, such as the writings of Babeuf and others.

The first direct attempts of the proletariat to attain its own ends—made in times of universal excitement, when feudal society was being overthrown—necessarily failed, owing to the then undeveloped state of the proletariat as well as to the absence of the economic conditions for its emancipation, conditions that had yet to be produced and could be produced by the impending bourgeois epoch alone. The revolutionary literature that accompanied these first movements of the proletariat had necessarily a reactionary character. It inculcated universal asceticism and social leveling in its crudest form.

The Socialist and Communist systems properly so called, those of St. Simon, Fourier, Owen and others, spring into existence in the early undeveloped period, described above, of the struggle between proletariat and bourgeoisie (see Section I. Bourgeois and Proletarians).

The founders of these systems indeed see the class antagonisms as well as the action of the decomposing elements in the prevailing form of society. But the proletariat, as yet in its infancy, offers to them the spectacle of a class without any historical initiative or any independent political movement.

Since the development of class antagonism keeps even pace with the development of industry, the economic situation, as they find it, does not as yet offer to them the material conditions for the emancipation of the proletariat. They therefore search after a new social science, after new social laws, that are to create these conditions.

Historical action is to yield to their personal inventive action, historically created conditions of emancipation to fantastic ones, and the gradual, spontaneous class organization of the proletariat to an organization of society specially contrived by these inventors. Future history resolves itself, in their eyes, into the propaganda and the practical carrying out of their social plans.

In the formation of their plans they are conscious of caring chiefly for the interests of the working class, as being the most suffering class. Only from the point of view of being the most suffering class does the proletariat exist for them.

The undeveloped state of the class struggle, as well as their own surroundings, causes Socialists of this kind to consider themselves far superior to all class antagonisms. They want to improve the condition of every member of society, even that of the most favored. Hence, they habitually appeal to society at large, without distinction of class; nay, by preference, to the ruling class. For how can people, when once they understand their system, fail to see in it the best possible plan of the best possible state of society?

Hence, they reject all political, and especially all revolutionary action; they wish to attain their ends by peaceful means, and endeavor by small experiments, necessarily doomed to failure, and by the force of example to pave the way for the new social Gospel.

Such fantastic pictures of future society, painted at a time when the proletariat is still in a very undeveloped state and has but a fantastic conception of its own position, correspond with the first instinctive yearnings of that class for a general reconstruction of society.

But these Socialist and Communist publications contain also a critical element. They attack every principle of existing society. Hence they are full of the most valuable materials for the enlightenment of the working class. The practical measures proposed in them—such as the abolition of the distinction between town and country, of the family, of the carrying on of industries for the account of private individuals, and of the wage system; the proclamation of social harmony, the conversion of the functions of the State into a mere superintendence of productions— all these proposals point solely to the disappearance of class antagonisms which were at that time only just cropping up, and which in these publications are recognized in their earliest indistinct and undefined forms only. These proposals, therefore, are of a purely Utopian character.

The significance of Critical-Utopian Socialism and Communism bears an inverse relation to historical development. In proportion as the modern class struggle develops and takes definite shape, this fantastic standing apart from the contest, these fantastic attacks on it, lose all practical value and all theoretical justification. Therefore, although the originators of these systems were in many respects revolutionary, their disciples in every case have formed mere reactionary sects. They hold fast by the original views of their masters, in opposition to the progressive historical development of the proletariat. They, therefore, endeavor, and that consistently, to deaden the class struggle and to reconcile the class antagonisms. They still dream of experimental realization of their social Utopias, of founding isolated *"phalanstères,"* of establishing "Home Colonies," of setting up a "Little Icaria"*—duodecimo editions of the New Jerusalem—and to realize all these castles in the air, they are compelled to appeal to the feelings and purses of the bourgeois. By degrees they sink into the category of the reactionary conservative Socialists depicted above, differing from these only by more systematic pedantry, and by their fanatical and superstitious belief in the miraculous effects of their social science.

They, therefore, violently oppose all political action on the part of the working class; such action, according to them, can only result from blind unbelief in the new Gospel.

The Owenites in England, and the Fourierists in France, respectively oppose the Chartists and the *Réformistes.*[6]

---

* *Phalanstères* were Socialist colonies on the plan of Charles Fourier; *Icaria* was the name given by Cabet to his Utopia and, later on, to his American communist colony. [*1888*]

"Home colonies" were what Owen called his Communist model societies. *Phalanstères* was the name of the public palaces planned by Fourier. *Icaria* was the name given to the Utopian land of fancy, whose Communist institutions Cabet portrayed. [*1890*]

IV. POSITION OF THE COMMUNISTS IN RELATION TO THE VARIOUS EXISTING OPPOSITION PARTIES

Section II has made clear the relations of the Communists to the existing working-class parties, such as the Chartists in England and the Agrarian Reformers in America.[1]

The Communists fight for the attainment of the immediate aims, for the enforcement of the momentary interests of the working class; but in the movement of the present, they also represent and take care of the future of that movement. In France the Communists ally themselves with the Social-Democrats* against the conservative and radical bourgeoisie, reserving, however, the right to take up a critical position in regard to phrases and illusions traditionally handed down from the great Revolution.

In Switzerland they support the Radicals, without losing sight of the fact that this party consists of antagonistic elements, partly of Democratic Socialists, in the French sense, partly of radical bourgeois.[3]

In Poland they support the party that insists on an agrarian revolution as the prime condition for national emancipation, that party which fomented the insurrection of Cracow in 1846.[4]

---

* The party then represented in Parliament by Ledru-Rollin, in literature by Louis Blanc,[2] in the daily press by *La Réforme*. The name of Social-Democracy signified, with these its inventors, a section of the Democratic or Republican party more or less tinged with socialism. [*1888*]

The party in France which at that time called itself Socialist-Democratic was represented in political life by Ledru-Rollin and in literature by Louis Blanc; thus it differed immeasurably from present-day German Social-Democracy. [*1890*]

In Germany they fight with the bourgeoisie whenever it acts in a revolutionary way, against the absolute monarchy, the feudal squirearchy, and the petty bourgeoisie.

But they never cease, for a single instant, to instil into the working class the clearest possible recognition of the hostile antagonism between bourgeoisie and proletariat in order that the German workers may straightway use, as so many weapons against the bourgeoisie, the social and political conditions that the bourgeoisie must necessarily introduce along with its supremacy, and in order that after the fall of the reactionary classes in Germany the fight against the bourgeoisie itself may immediately begin.

The Communists turn their attention chiefly to Germany, because that country is on the eve of a bourgeois revolution that is bound to be carried out under more advanced conditions of European civilization, and with a much more developed proletariat than that of England in the 17th, and of France in the 18th century, and because the bourgeois revolution in Germany will be but the prelude to an immediately following proletarian revolution.

In short, the Communists everywhere support every revolutionary movement against the existing social and political order of things.

In all these movements they bring to the front, as the leading question in each, the property question, no matter what its degree of development at the time.

Finally, they labor everywhere for the union and agreement of the democratic parties of all countries.

The Communists disdain to conceal their views and aims. They openly declare that their ends can be attained only by the forcible overthrow of all existing social conditions. Let the ruling classes tremble at a Communistic revolution. The proletarians have nothing to lose but their chains. They have a world to win.

WORKING MEN OF ALL COUNTRIES, UNITE!

Fighting in the St. Antoine district of Paris, June 1848. *Lithograph by De Schamos.*

PART THREE

PREFACES BY MARX AND ENGELS

A spinning mill in England, around 1850.

PREFACES BY MARX AND ENGELS

GERMAN EDITION OF 1872

The Communist League, an international association of workers, which could of course be only a secret one under the conditions obtaining at the time, commissioned the undersigned, at the Congress held in London in November 1847, to draw up for publication a detailed theoretical and practical program of the Party. Such was the origin of the following *Manifesto,* the manuscript of which traveled to London, to be printed a few weeks before the February Revolution. First published in German, it has been republished in that language in at least twelve different editions in Germany, England and America. It was published in English for the first time in 1850 in the *Red Republican,*[1] London, translated by Miss Helen Macfarlane, and in 1871 in at least three different translations in America. A French version first appeared in Paris shortly before the June insurrection of 1848 and recently in *Le Socialiste* of New York.[2] A new translation is in the course of preparation. A Polish version appeared in London shortly after it was first published in German. A Russian translation was published in Geneva in the sixties.[3] Into Danish, too, it was translated shortly after its first appearance.

However much the state of things may have altered during the last twenty-five years, the general principles laid down in this *Manifesto* are, on the whole, as correct today as ever. Here and there some detail might be improved. The practical application of the principles will depend, as the *Manifesto* itself states, everywhere and at all times on the historical conditions for the time being existing, and for that reason no special stress is laid on the revolutionary measures proposed at the end of Section II. That passage would, in many respects, be very differently worded today. In view of the gigantic strides of Modern Industry in the last twenty-five years, and of the accompanying improved and extended party organization of the working class, in view of the practical experience gained, first in the February Revolution, and then still more in the Paris Commune, where the proletariat for the first time held political power for two whole months, this program has in some details become antiquated. One thing especially was proved by the Commune, viz., that "the working class cannot simply lay hold of the ready-made state machinery, and wield it for its own purposes." (See *The Civil War in France; Address of the General Council of the International Working Men's Association,* London, Truelove, 1871, p. 15,[4] where this point is further developed.) Further, it is self-evident that the criticism of Socialist literature is deficient in relation to the present time because it comes down only to 1847; also, that the remarks on the relation of the Communists to the various opposition parties (Section IV), although in principle still correct, yet in practice are antiquated because the political situation has been entirely changed, and the progress of history has swept from off the earth the greater portion of the political parties there enumerated.

But, then, the *Manifesto* has become a historical document which we have no longer any right to alter. A subsequent edition may perhaps appear with an introduction bridging the gap from 1847 to the present day; this reprint was too unexpected to leave us time for that.

London, June 24, 1872

KARL MARX
FREDERICK ENGELS

RUSSIAN EDITION OF 1882[1]

The first Russian edition of the *Manifesto of the Communist Party,* translated by Bakunin, was published early in the sixties by the printing office of the *Kolokol.* Then the West could see in it (the *Russian* edition of the *Manifesto*) only a literary curiosity. Such a view would be impossible today.

What a limited field the proletarian movement still occupied at that time (December 1847) is most clearly shown by the last section of the *Manifesto:* the position of the Communists in relation to the various opposition parties in the various countries. Precisely Russia and the United States are missing here. It was the time when Russia constituted the last great reserve of all European reaction, when the United States absorbed the surplus proletarian forces of Europe through immigration. Both countries provided Europe with raw materials and were at the same time markets for the sale of its industrial products. At that time both were, therefore, in one way or another pillars of the existing European order.

How very different today! Precisely European immigration fitted North America for a gigantic agricultural production, whose competition is shaking the very foundations of European landed property, large and small. In addition it enabled the United States to exploit its tremendous industrial resources with an energy and on a scale that must shortly break the industrial monopoly of Western Europe, and especially of England, existing up to now. Both circumstances react in revolutionary manner upon America itself. Step by step the small and middle landownership of the farmers, the basis of the whole political constitution, is succumbing to the competition of giant farms; simultaneously, a mass proletariat and a fabulous concentration of capitals are developing for the first time in the industrial regions.

And now Russia? During the Revolution of 1848–49 not only the European princes, but the European bourgeois as well, found their only salvation from the proletariat, just beginning to awaken, in Russian intervention. The Tsar was proclaimed the chief of European reaction. Today he is a prisoner of war of the revolution, in Gatchina,[2] and Russia forms the vanguard of revolutionary action in Europe.

The *Communist Manifesto* had as its object the proclamation of the inevitably impending dissolution of modern bourgeois property. But in Russia we find, face to face with the rapidly developing capitalist swindle and bourgeois landed property, just beginning to develop, more than half the land owned in common by the peasants. Now the question is: can the Russian *obshchina*,[3] though greatly undermined, yet a form of the primeval common ownership of land, pass directly to the higher form of communist common ownership? Or on the contrary, must it first pass through the same process of dissolution as constitutes the historical evolution of the West?

The only answer to that possible today is this: If the Russian Revolution becomes the signal for a proletarian revolution in the West, so that both complement each other, the present Russian common ownership of land may serve as the starting point for a communist development.

London, January 21, 1882

KARL MARX
FREDERICK ENGELS

GERMAN EDITION OF 1883[1]

The preface to the present edition I must, alas, sign alone. Marx, the man to whom the whole working class of Europe and America owes more than to anyone else, rests at Highgate Cemetery and over his grave the first grass is already growing. Since his death, there can be even less thought of revising or supplementing the *Manifesto*. All the more do I consider it necessary again to state here the following expressly:

The basic thought running through the *Manifesto*—that economic production and the structure of society of every historical epoch necessarily arising therefrom constitute the foundation for the political and intellectual history of that epoch; that consequently (ever since the dissolution of the primeval communal ownership of land) all history has been a history of class struggles, of struggles between exploited and exploiting, between dominated and dominating classes at various stages of social development; that this struggle, however, has now reached a stage where the exploited and oppressed class (the proletariat) can no longer emancipate itself from the class which exploits and oppresses it (the bourgeoisie), without at the same time for ever freeing the whole of society from exploitation, oppression and class struggles—this basic throught belongs solely and exclusively to Marx.*

I have already stated this many times; but precisely now it is necessary that it also stand in front of the *Manifesto* itself.
London, June 28, 1883

F. ENGELS

ENGLISH EDITION OF 1888[1]

The *Manifesto* was published as the platform of the Communist League, a workingmen's association, first exclusively German, later on international, and under the political conditions of the Continent before 1848 unavoidably a secret society. At a Congress of the League, held in London in November 1847, Marx and Engels were commissioned to prepare for publication a complete theoretical and practical party program. Drawn up in German, in January 1848, the manuscript was sent to the printer in London a few weeks before the French revolution of February 24. A French translation was brought out in Paris, shortly before the insurrection of June 1848. The first English translation, by Miss Helen Macfarlane, appeared in George Julian Harney's *Red Republican,* London, 1850. A Danish and a Polish edition had also been published.

The defeat of the Parisian insurrection of June 1848—the first great battle between Proletariat and Bourgeoisie—drove again into the background, for a time, the social and political aspira-

---

* "This proposition," I wrote in the preface to the English translation, "which, in my opinion, is destined to do for history what Darwin's theory has done for biology, we, both of us, had been gradually approaching for some years before 1845. How far I had independently progressed toward it, is best shown by my *Condition of the Working Class in England.* But when I again met Marx at Brussels in spring, 1845, he had it ready worked out, and put it before me in terms almost as clear as those in which I have stated it here." *[1890]*

tions of the European working class. Thenceforth, the struggle for supremacy was again, as it had been before the revolution of February, solely between different sections of the propertied class; the working class was reduced to a fight for political elbow-room, and to the position of extreme wing of the middle-class Radicals. Wherever independent proletarian movements continued to show signs of life, they were ruthlessly hunted down. Thus the Prussian police hunted out the Central Board of the Communist League, then located in Cologne. The members were arrested and, after eighteen months' imprisonment, they were tried in October 1852. This celebrated "Cologne Communist trial" lasted from October 4 till November 12; seven of the prisoners were sentenced to terms of imprisonment in a fortress, varying from three to six years. Immediately after the sentence, the League was formally dissolved by the remaining members. As to the *Manifesto,* it seemed thenceforth to be doomed to oblivion.

When the European working class had recovered sufficient strength for another attack on the ruling classes, the International Working Men's Association sprang up. But this association, formed with the express aim of welding into one body the whole militant proletariat of Europe and America, could not at once proclaim the principles laid down in the *Manifesto.* The International was bound to have a program broad enough to be acceptable to the English Trades' Unions, to the followers of Proudhon in France, Belgium, Italy and Spain, and to the Lassalleans* in Germany. Marx, who drew up this program to the satisfaction of all parties, entirely trusted to the intellectual development of the working class which was sure to result from combined action and mutual discussion. The very events and vicissitudes of the struggle against Capital, the defeats even more than the victories, could not help bringing home to men's minds the insufficiency of their various favorite nostrums, and prepar-

---

* Lassalle[2] personally, to us, always acknowledged himself to be a disciple of Marx, and, as such, stood on the ground of the *Manifesto.* But in his public agitation, 1862–64, he did not go beyond demanding cooperative workshops supported by state credit.

ing the way for a more complete insight into the true conditions of working-class emancipation. And Marx was right. The International, on its breaking up in 1874, left the workers quite different men from what it had found them in 1864. Proudhonism in France, Lassalleanism in Germany were dying out, and even the Conservative English Trades' Unions, though most of them had long since severed their connection with the International, were gradually advancing toward that point at which, last year at Swansea, their President could say in their name, "Continental Socialism has lost its terrors for us." In fact, the principles of the *Manifesto* had made considerable headway among the working men of all countries.

The *Manifesto* itself thus came to the front again. The German text had been, since 1850, reprinted several times in Switzerland, England and America. In 1872, it was translated into English in New York, where the translation was published in *Woodhull and Claflin's Weekly*. From this English version, a French one was made in *Le Socialiste* of New York. Since then at least two more English translations, more or less mutilated, have been brought out in America, and one of them has been reprinted in England. The first Russian translation, made by Bakunin, was published at Herzen's *Kolokol* office in Geneva, about 1863; a second one, by the heroic Vera Zasulich,[3] also in Geneva, 1882. A new Danish edition is to be found in *Social-demokratisk Bibliothek*, Copenhagen, 1885; a fresh French translation in *Le Socialiste*, Paris, 1885. From this latter a Spanish version was prepared and published in Madrid, 1886. Not counting the German reprints, there have been at least twelve editions. An Armenian translation, which was to be published in Constantinople some months ago, did not see the light, I am told, because the publisher was afraid of bringing out a book with the name of Marx on it, while the translator declined to call it his own production. Of further translations into other languages I have heard, but have not seen them. Thus the history of the *Manifesto* reflects to a great extent the history of the modern working-class movement; at present it is undoubtedly the most widespread, the most international production of all Socialist literature, the common platform acknowledged by millions of workingmen from Siberia to California.

Yet, when it was written we could not have called it a *Socialist* Manifesto. By Socialists, in 1847, were understood, on the one hand, the adherents of the various utopian systems: Owenites in England, Fourierists in France, both of them already reduced to the position of mere sects, and gradually dying out; on the other hand, the most multifarious social quacks, who by all manners of tinkering professed to redress, without any danger to capital and profit, all sorts of social grievances, in both cases men outside the working-class movement and looking rather to the "educated" classes for support. Whatever portion of the working class had become convinced of the insufficiency of mere political revolutions and had proclaimed the necessity of a total social change, that portion then called itself Communist. It was a crude, rough-hewn, purely instinctive sort of Communism; still, it touched the cardinal point and was powerful enough amongst the working class to produce the Utopian Communism in France of Cabet, and in Germany of Weitling. Thus in 1847 Socialism was a middle-class movement, Communism a working-class movement. Socialism was, on the Continent at least, "respectable"; Communism was the very opposite. And as our notion from the very beginning was that "the emancipation of the working class must be the act of the working class itself," there could be no doubt as to which of the two names we must take. Moreover, we have, ever since, been far from repudiating it.

The *Manifesto* being our joint production, I consider myself bound to state that the fundamental proposition which forms its nucleus belongs to Marx. That proposition is: that in every historical epoch, the prevailing mode of economic production and exchange, and the social organization necessarily following from it, form the basis upon which is built up, and from which alone can be explained, the political and intellectual history of that epoch; that consequently the whole history of mankind (since the dissolution of primitive tribal society, holding land in common ownership) has been a history of class struggles, contests between exploiting and exploited, ruling and oppressed classes; that the history of these class struggles forms a series of evolutions in which, nowadays, a stage has been reached where the exploited and oppressed class—the proletariat—cannot attain its emancipation from the sway of the exploiting and ruling class—the bourgeoisie —without at the same time, and once and for all, emancipating society at large from all exploitation, oppression, class distinctions and class struggles.

This proposition which, in my opinion, is destined to do for history what Darwin's theory has done for biology, we, both of us, had been gradually approaching for some years before 1845. How far I had independently progressed toward it, is best shown by my *Condition of the Working Class in England*. But when I again met Marx at Brussels, in spring, 1845, he had it ready worked out, and put it before me in terms almost as clear as those in which I have stated it here.

From our joint preface to the German edition of 1872, I quote the following:

[*Here Engels quotes the second paragraph and the first sentence of the third paragraph of this preface, see above. Then he continues:*]

The present translation is by Mr. Samuel Moore, the translator of the greater portion of Marx's *Capital*. We have revised it in common, and I have added a few notes explanatory of historical allusions.

London, January 30, 1888   FREDERICK ENGELS

GERMAN EDITION OF 1890

Since the above was written, a new German edition[1] of the *Manifesto* has again become necessary, and much has also happened to the *Manifesto* which should be recorded here.

A second Russian translation—by Vera Zasulich—appeared at Geneva in 1882; the preface to that edition was written by Marx and myself. Unfortunately, the original German manuscript has gone astray; I must therefore retranslate from the Russian, which will in no way improve the text. It reads:

[*Here Engels quotes the preface to this edition, see above. Then he continues:*] At about the same date, a new Polish version appeared in Geneva, *Manifest Komunistyczny.*

Furthermore, a new Danish translation has appeared in the *Social-demokratisk Bibliothek,* Kjöbenhavn, 1885. Unfortunately it is not quite complete; certain essential passages, which seem to have presented difficulties to the translator, have been omitted, and in addition there are signs of carelessness here and there, which are all the more unpleasantly conspicuous since the translation indicates that had the translator taken a little more pains he would have done an excellent piece of work.

A new French version appeared in 1885 in *Le Socialiste* of Paris; it is the best published to date.

From this latter a Spanish version was published the same year, first in *El Socialista* of Madrid, and then reissued in pamphlet form: *Manifiesto del Partido Comunista* por Carlos Marx y F. Engels, Madrid, Administración de *El Socialista,* Hernán Cortés 8.

As a matter of curiosity I may also mention that in 1887 the manuscript of an Armenian translation was offered to a publisher in Constantinople. But the good man did not have the courage to publish something bearing the name of Marx and suggested that the translator set down his own name as author, which the latter, however, declined.

After one and then another of the more or less inaccurate American translations had been repeatedly reprinted in England, an authentic version at last appeared in 1888. This was by my friend Samuel Moore, and we went through it together once more before it was sent to press. It is entitled: *Manifesto of the Communist Party,* by Karl Marx and Frederick Engels. Authorized English Translation, edited and annotated by Frederick Engels. 1888. London, William Reeves, 185 Fleet st., E. C. I have added some of the notes of that edition to the present one.

The *Manifesto* has had a history of its own. Greeted with enthusiasm at the time of its appearance by the then still not at all numerous vanguard of scientific Socialism (as it proved by the translations mentioned in the first preface), it was soon forced into the background by the reaction that began with the defeat of the Paris workers in June 1848, and was finally excommunicated "according to law" by the conviction of the Cologne Communists in November 1852. With the disappearance from the public scene of the workers' movement that had begun with the February Revolution, the *Manifesto* too passed into the background.

When the working class of Europe had again gathered sufficient strength for a new onslaught upon the power of the ruling classes, the International Working Men's Association came into being. Its aim was to weld together into *one* huge army the whole militant working class of Europe and America. Therefore it could not *set out* from the principles laid down in the *Manifesto*. It was bound to have a program which would not shut the door on the English trade unions, the French, Belgian, Italian and Spanish Proudhonists and the German Lassalleans.* This program—the preamble to the Rules of the International—was drawn up by Marx with a master hand acknowledged even by Bakunin and the Anarchists. For the ultimate triumph of the ideas set forth in the *Manifesto* Marx relied solely and exclusively upon the intellectual development of the working class, as it necessarily had to ensue from united action and discussion. The events and vicissitudes in the struggle against capital, the defeats even more than the successes, could not but demonstrate to the fighters the inadequacy hitherto of their universal panaceas and make their minds more receptive to a thorough understanding of the true conditions for the emancipation of the workers. And Marx was right. The working class of 1874, at the dissolution of the International, was altogether different from that of 1864, at its foundation. Proudhonism in the Latin countries and the specific Lassalleanism in Germany were dying out, and even the then arch-conservative English trade unions were grad-

---

* Lassalle personally, to us, always acknowledged himself to be a "disciple" of Marx, and, as such, stood, of course, on the ground of the *Manifesto*. Matters were quite different with regard to those of his followers who did not go beyond his demand for producers' cooperatives supported by state credits and who divided the whole working class into supporters of state assistance and supporters of self-assistance.

ually approaching the point where in 1887 the chairman of their Swansea Congress could say in their name, "Continental Socialism has lost its terrors for us." Yet by 1887 Continental Socialism was almost exclusively the theory heralded in the *Manifesto*. Thus, to a certain extent, the history of the *Manifesto* reflects the history of the modern working-class movement since 1848. At present it is doubtless the most widely circulated, the most international product of all Socialist literature, the common program of many millions of workers of all countries, from Siberia to California.

Nevertheless, when it appeared we could not have called it a *Socialist* Manifesto. In 1847 two kinds of people were considered Socialists. On the one hand were the adherents of the various Utopian systems, notably the Owenites in England and the Fourierists in France, both of whom at that date had already dwindled to mere sects gradually dying out. On the other, the manifold types of social quacks who wanted to eliminate social abuses through their various universal panaceas and all kinds of patchwork, without hurting capital and profit in the least. In both cases, people who stood outside the labor movement and who looked for support rather to the "educated" classes. The section of the working class, however, which demanded a radical reconstruction of society, convinced that mere political revolutions were not enough, then called itself *Communist*. It was still a rough-hewn, only instinctive, and frequently somewhat crude Communism. Yet it was powerful enough to bring into being two systems of Utopian Communism—in France the "Icarian" Communism of Cabet, and in Germany that of Weitling. Socialism in 1847 signified a bourgeois movement, Communism, a working-class movement. Socialism was, on the Continent at least, quite respectable, whereas Communism was the very opposite. And since we were very decidedly of the opinion as early as then that "the emancipation of the workers must be the act of the working class itself," we could have no hesitation as to which of the two names we should choose. Nor has it ever occurred to us since to repudiate it.

"Working men of all countries, unite!" But few voices responded when we proclaimed these words to the world forty-two years ago, on the eve of the first Paris Revolution in which the proletariat came out with demands of its own. On September 28, 1864, however, the proletarians of most of the Western European countries joined hands in the International Working Men's Association of glorious memory. True, the International itself lived only nine years. But that the eternal union of the proletarians of all countries created by it is still alive and lives stronger than ever, there is no better witness than this day. Because today, as I write these lines, the European and American proletariat is reviewing its fighting forces, mobilized for the first time, mobilized as *one* army, under *one* flag, for *one* immediate aim: the standard eight-hour working day, to be established by legal enactment, as proclaimed by the Geneva Congress of the International in 1866, and again by the Paris Workers' Congress in 1889. And today's spectacle will open the eyes of the capitalists and landlords of all countries to the fact that today the working men of all countries are united indeed.

If only Marx were still by my side to see this with his own eyes!

London, May 1, 1890   F. Engels

POLISH EDITION OF 1892

The fact that a new Polish edition[1] of the *Communist Manifesto* has become necessary gives rise to various thoughts.

First of all, it is noteworthy that of late the *Manifesto* has become an index, as it were, of the development of large-scale industry on the European continent. In proportion as large-scale industry expands in a given country, the demand grows among the workers of that country for enlightenment regarding their position as the working class in relation to the possessing classes, the socialist movement spreads among them and the demand for the *Manifesto* increases. Thus, not only the state of the labor movement but also the degree of development of large-scale industry can be measured with fair accuracy in every country by the number of copies of the *Manifesto* circulated in the language of that country.

Accordingly, the new Polish edition indicates a decided progress of Polish industry. And there can be no doubt whatever that this progress since the previous edition published ten years ago has actually taken place. Russian Poland, Congress Poland, has become the big industrial region of the Russian Empire. Whereas Russian large-scale industry is scattered sporadically— a part around the Gulf of Finland, another in the center (Moscow and Vladimir), a third along the coasts of the Black and Azov seas, and still others elsewhere—Polish industry has been packed into a relatively small area and enjoys both the advantages and the disadvantages arising from such concentration. The competing Russian manufacturers acknowledged the advantages when they demanded protective tariffs against Poland, in spite of their ardent desire to transform the Poles into Russians. The disadvantages—for the Polish manufacturers and the Russian government—are manifest in the rapid spread of socialist ideas among the Polish workers and in the growing demand for the *Manifesto*.

But the rapid development of Polish industry, outstripping that of Russia, is in its turn a new proof of the inexhaustible vitality of the Polish people and a new guarantee of its impending national restoration. And the restoration of an independent strong Poland is a matter which concerns not only the Poles but all of us. A sincere international collaboration of the European nations is possible only if each of these nations is fully autonomous in its own house. The Revolution of 1848, which under the banner of the proletariat, after all, merely let the proletarian fighters do the work of the bourgeoisie, also secured the independence of Italy, Germany and Hungary through its testamentary executors, Louis Bonaparte and Bismarck; but Poland, which since 1792 had done more for the Revolution than all these three together, was left to its own resources when it succumbed in 1863 to a tenfold greater Russian force. The nobility could neither maintain nor regain Polish independence; today, to the bourgeoisie, this independence is, to say the least, immaterial. Nevertheless, it is a necessity for the harmonious collaboration of the European nations. It can be gained only by the young Polish proletariat, and in its hands it is secure. For the workers of all the rest of Europe need the independence of Poland just as much as the Polish workers themselves.

London, February 10, 1892

F. ENGELS

ITALIAN EDITION OF 1893[1]

TO THE ITALIAN READER

Publication of the *Manifesto of the Communist Party* coincided, one may say, with March 18, 1848, the day of the revolutions in Milan and Berlin, which were armed uprisings of the two nations situated in the center, the one, of the continent of Europe, the other of the Mediterranean; two nations until then enfeebled by division and internal strife and thus fallen under foreign domination. While Italy was subject to the Emperor of Austria, Germany underwent the yoke, not less effective though more indirect, of the Tsar of all the Russias. The consequences of March 18, 1848 freed both Italy and Germany from this disgrace; if from 1848 to 1871 these two great nations were reconstituted and somehow again put on their own, it was, as Karl Marx used to say, because the men who suppressed the Revolution of 1848 were, nevertheless, its testamentary executors in spite of themselves.

Everywhere that revolution was the work of the working class; it was the latter that built the barricades and paid with its lifeblood. Only the Paris workers, in overthrowing the government, had the very definite intention of overthrowing the bourgeois regime. But conscious though they were of the fatal antagonism existing between their own class and the bourgeoisie, still neither the economic progress of the country nor the intellectual development of the mass of French workers had as yet reached the stage which would have made a social reconstruction possible. In the final analysis, therefore, the fruits of the revolution were reaped by the capitalist class. In the other countries, in Italy, in Germany, in Austria, the workers from the very outset did nothing but raise the bourgeoisie to power. But in any country the rule of the bourgeoisie is impossible without national independence. Therefore, the Revolution of 1848 had to bring in its train the unity and autonomy of the nations that had lacked them up to then: Italy, Germany, Hungary. Poland will follow in turn.

Thus, if the Revolution of 1848 was not a socialist revolution, it paved the way, prepared the ground for the latter. Through the impetus given to large-scale industry in all countries, the bourgeois regime during the last forty-five years has everywhere created a numerous, concentrated and powerful proletariat. It has thus raised, to use the language of the *Manifesto,* its own grave-diggers. Without restoring autonomy and unity to each nation, it will be impossible to achieve the international union of the proletariat, or the peaceful and intelligent cooperation of these nations toward common aims. Just imagine joint international action by the Italian, Hungarian, German, Polish and Russian workers under the political conditions preceding 1848!

The battles fought in 1848 were thus not fought in vain. Nor have the forty-five years separating us from that revolutionary epoch passed to no purpose. The fruits are ripening, and all I wish is that the publication of this Italian translation may augur as well for the victory of the Italian proletariat as the publication of the original did for the international revolution.

The *Manifesto* does full justice to the revolutionary part played by capitalism in the past. The first capitalist nation was Italy. The close of the feudal Middle Ages and the opening of the modern capitalist era are marked by a colossal figure: an Italian, Dante, both the last poet of the Middle Ages and the first poet of modern times. Today, as in 1300, a new historical era is approaching. Will Italy give us the new Dante, who will mark the hour of birth of this new, proletarian era?

London, February 1, 1893

FREDERICK ENGELS

PART FOUR

APPENDICES

THE RED REPUBLICAN.

EQUALITY, LIBERTY, FRATERNITY.

EDITED BY G. JULIAN HARNEY.

No. 21.—Vol. I.] SATURDAY, NOVEMBER 9, 1850. [Price One Penny.

German Communism.

MANIFESTO OF THE GERMAN COMMUNIST PARTY.

(Published in February, 1848.)

THE following Manifesto, which has since been adopted by all fractions of German Communists, was drawn up in the German language, in January 1848, by Citizens *Charles Marx* and *Frederic Engels*. It was immediately printed in London, in the German language, and published a few days before the outbreak of the Revolution of February. The turmoil consequent upon that great event made it impossible to carry out, at that time, the intention of translating it into all the languages of civilized Europe. There exist two different French versions of it in manuscript, but under the present oppressive laws of France, the publication of either of them has been found impracticable. The English reader will be enabled, by the following excellent translation of this important document, to judge of the plans and principles of the most advanced party of the German Revolutionists.

It must not be forgotten, that the whole of this Manifesto was written and printed before the Revolution of February.

A frightful hobgoblin stalks throughout Europe. We are haunted by a ghost, the ghost of Communism. All the Powers of the Past have joined in a holy crusade to lay this ghost to rest,—the Pope and the Czar, Metternich and Guizot, French Radicals and German police agents. Where is the opposition which has not been accused of Communism by its enemies in Power? And where the opposition that has not hurled this blighting accusation at the heads of the more advanced oppositionists, as well as at those of its official enemies?

Two things appear on considering these facts. I. The ruling Powers of Europe acknowledge Communism to be also a Power. II. It is time for the Communists to lay before the world an account of their aims and tendencies, and to oppose these silly fables about the bugbear of Communism, by a manifesto of the Communist Party.

CHAPTER I.

BOURGEOIS AND PROLETARIANS.

HITHERTO the history of Society has been the history of the battles between the classes composing it. Freemen and Slaves, Patricians and Plebeians, Nobles and Serfs, Members of Guilds and journeymen,—in a word, the oppressors and the oppressed, have always stood in direct opposition to each other. The battle between them has sometimes been open, sometimes concealed, but always continuous. A never-ceasing battle, which has invariably ended, either in a revolutionary alteration of the social system, or in the common destruction of the hostile classes.

In the earlier historical epochs we find almost everywhere a minute division of Society into classes or ranks, a variety of grades in social position. In ancient Rome we find Patricians, Knights, Plebeians, Slaves; in mediæval Europe, Feudal Lords, Vassals, Burghers, Journeymen, Serfs; and in each of these classes there were again grades and distinctions. Modern Bourgeois Society, which proceeded from the ruins of the feudal system, but the Bourgeois régime has not abolished the antagonism of classes.

New classes, new conditions of oppression, new forms and modes of carrying on the struggle, have been substituted for the old ones. The characteristic of our Epoch, the Era of the Middle-class, or Bourgeoisie, is that the struggle between the various Social Classes, has been reduced to its simplest form. Society incessantly tends to be divided into two great camps, into two great hostile armies, the Bourgeoisie and the Proletariat. The burgesses of the early Communes sprang from the Serfs of the Middle Ages, and from this Municipal class were developed the primitive elements of the modern Bourgeoisie. The discovery of the New World, the circumnavigation of Africa, gave the Middleclass—then coming into being—new fields of action. The colonization of America, the opening up of the East Indian and Chinese Markets, the Colonial Trade, the increase of commodities generally and of the means of exchange, gave an impetus, hitherto unknown, to Commerce, Shipping, and Manufactures; and aided the rapid evolution of the revolutionary element in the old decaying, feudal form of Society. The old feudal way of managing the industrial interest by means of guilds and monopolies was not found sufficient for the increased demand caused by the opening up of these new markets. It was replaced by the manufacturing system. Guilds vanished before the industrial Middle-class, and the division of labour between the different corporations was succeeded by the division of labour between the workmen of one and the same great workshop.

But the demand always increased, new markets came into play. The manufacturing system, in its turn, was found to be inadequate. At this point industrial Production was revolutionised by machinery and steam. The modern industrial system was developed in all its gigantic proportions; instead of the industrial Middle-class we find industrial millionaires, chiefs of whole industrial armies, the modern Bourgeois, or Middle-class Capitalists. The discovery of America was the first step towards the formation of a colossal market, embracing the whole world; whereby an immense development was given to Commerce, and to the means of communication by sea and land. This again reacted upon the industrial system, and the developement of the Bourgeoisie, the increase of their Capital, the superseding of all classes handed down to modern times from the Middle Ages, kept pace with the developement of Production, Trade, and Steam communication.

We find, therefore, that the modern Bourgeoisie are themselves the result of a long process of developement, of a series of revolutions in the modes of Production and Exchange. Each of the degrees of industrial evolution, passed through by the modern Middle-class, was accompanied by a corresponding

---

The opening of the English translation of the *Communist Manifesto,* as published in *The Red Republican,* November 9, 1850. The authors are given as "Citizens Charles Marx and Frederic Engels." It begins "A frightful hobgoblin stalks throughout Europe. . . ."

I. MARX AND ENGELS ON THE HISTORY OF THE COMMUNIST LEAGUE

Both Marx and Engels have left an account of the Communist League as they later remembered it. That of Marx can be found in his *Karl Vogt,*[1] 1860; he called it "half forgotten stories buried a long time"—proof of how little interest existed in those days, when the labor movement had nowhere on the Continent recovered from the defeat of 1848–49.

Engels' account is much later. We find it in his Introduction to the third edition of Marx's *Enthüllungen über den Kommunisten Prozess zu Köln* (Revelations Concerning the Communist Trial in Cologne), which appeared in 1885.[2] This trial took place in 1852 (See Note 2, Section V, Introduction) and resulted in a number of convictions obtained by the now familiar methods of spies, perjurers, etc., under the inspiration of the Prussian police superintendent Stieber. The pamphlet was originally published in the *New England Zeitung* of Boston in 1853, when a first edition, printed in Switzerland, had been confiscated after having been smuggled into Germany.

Both accounts rely on memory, and have been supplemented and corrected on details by documents since come to light.

1.

MARX'S ACCOUNT
(From *Karl Vogt*)

The Communist League was founded in 1836 in Paris, originally under another name. The organization, as it gradually developed, was the following: A certain number of members

147

formed a "community" *(Gemeinde)*, several communities in the same city a "circle" *(Kreis)*, a larger or smaller number of circles grouped themselves around a "leading circle"; at the head of the whole stood the "central committee," elected at a congress of deputies of all circles, but was authorized to complement itself and in urgent cases to appoint provisionally its successor. The seat of the central committee was first Paris; from 1840 to the beginning of 1848 it was London.

The leaders of the communities and circles were all, like the central committee itself, appointed by election. This democratic constitution, utterly unfit for conspiratorial secret societies, was at any rate not incompatible with the task of a propaganda society. The activity of the League consisted primarily in the foundation of open German workers' educational societies, and most societies of this kind, that still exist in Switzerland, England, Belgium and the United States, were founded either directly by the League or by former members. The constitution of these workers' societies was therefore everywhere the same. One day a week was devoted to discussion, another day to social entertainment (singing, declamations, etc.). Everywhere the societies founded libraries and, wherever possible, classes for the instruction of the workers in elementary fields of knowledge. The League, standing behind the open workers' societies and guiding them, found in them the immediate arena for public propaganda; from the ranks of the most efficient members of the workers' societies it could also do its recruiting. Because of the roving life of the German artisans it was only on rare occasions that the central committee had to send out special emissaries.

As to the secret doctrine of the League, this passed through all the varying forms of French and English socialism and communism, as well as their German variations (such as Weitling's fantasies). After 1839, the religious question dominated, next to the social one. Inside these workers' societies the different phases through which German philosophy passed from 1839 to 1846 were followed with the most lively partisanship. The work of the League—propaganda among the workers in Germany—

demanded that the secret form be continued. During my first stay in Paris* I used to be in personal contact with both the local leaders of the League and with the leaders of most French secret workers' societies, without joining any of them. In Brussels, to which city I had been exiled by Guizot, I founded with Engels, W. Wolff and others the still existing German Workers' Educational Society.

We published at the same time a series of pamphlets, partly printed, partly lithographed, in which we subjected the mixture of French-English socialism or communism and German philosophy, which at the time constituted the secret doctrine of the League, to a merciless criticism. We established in its stead the scientific understanding of the economic structure of bourgeois society as the only tenable theoretical foundation. We also explained in popular form that our task was not the fulfillment of some utopian system but the conscious participation in the historic process of social revolution that was taking place before our eyes.

This activity resulted in the London central committee entering into correspondence with us. At the end of 1846 it sent one of its members to Brussels to invite us to enter the League. This was the watchmaker Joseph Moll, who later lost his life on the Baden battlefield as a soldier of the revolution. Whatever objections we had against this proposal were defeated by Moll's statement that the central committee planned to call together a congress of the League at London. There the critical position we had taken would be accepted as the doctrine of the League in a public manifesto. Antiquated and objecting elements could only be counteracted by our personal collaboration, but this was only possible if we joined the League.

Hence we did join. The congress took place with League members from Switzerland, France, Belgium, Germany and England represented. After strenuous debates, lasting several weeks,[3] the *Manifesto of the Communist Party,* composed by Engels and me, was accepted.

* From the end of 1843 until early 1845.

2.

ENGELS' ACCOUNT[4]

In the year 1834 a group of German refugees in Paris founded a secret society known as the League of the Proscribed. The organization was democratic-republican. During 1836 the most extreme, most proletarian elements broke away and constituted themselves into a new secret League of the Just. The parent organization, to which only such sleepy-heads as Jakobus Venedey[5] remained faithful, soon fell into a profound slumber; by the year 1840, when the police routed out a few sections, it was the merest shadow of its former self. The new League, however, developed rather quickly. Originally it was a German outlyer of French working-class communism which was based mainly on Babouvist memories and which was taking definite shape and form about this time in Paris. Among these circles community of goods was demanded as the natural outcome of "equality." The aims of the Just were the same as those of the other Parisian secret societies of the period. The League was thus about equally divided between propaganda and conspiratorial work. Paris was always regarded as the focal point of revolutionary activity, although the preparation of occasional *Putsche* [revolutionary actions] in Germany was not excluded. Since, however, Paris was considered the place where the decisive battle would occur, the League in those days was in reality not much more than a German branch of the French secret societies, and especially of the Société des Saisons, led by Blanqui and Barbès. Indeed, the League was in such close touch with the Saisons that, when the French rose in revolt on May 12, 1839, the sections of the League marched shoulder to shoulder with them and thus suffered all together a common defeat.

From among the Germans Karl Schapper and Heinrich Bauer were arrested. The government of Louis Philippe was content to expel them from France after a long term in prison. Both men went to London. Schapper, from Weilburg in Nassau [W.

Germany], had been a student of forestry at Giessen and had, in 1832, participated in the conspiracy of Georg Büchner. On April 3, 1833 he took part in the storming of the constabulary station in Frankfurt. After this exploit he escaped abroad and in February 1834 joined Mazzini's forces in Savoy.[6] In physique a giant, resolute and energetic, always ready to sacrifice bourgeois existence and life, he was the prototype of the professional revolutionist of the eighteen-thirties. His development from "demagogue" to communist proves that, despite a certain obtuseness of thinking, he was nevertheless receptive to better theoretical understanding. Once convinced, he held tenaciously to his opinions, and precisely because of this his revolutionary passion sometimes overwhelmed his better judgment. Afterward he was always ready to acknowledge himself in the wrong. He was a man of genuine mettle all through, and his services to the foundation of the German labor movement will never be forgotten.

Heinrich Bauer came from Franconia. He was a shoemaker, a vivid, happy, witty little man whose small frame held a fund of shrewdness and determination.

Once established in London, Schapper, who had been a typesetter in Paris, now tried to earn his living as a teacher of languages. He and Bauer gathered up the broken threads of the League and made London the center of its activities. Joseph Moll joined their company (he may already have done so in Paris). He was a watchmaker from Cologne; was a medium-sized Hercules—how often have I seen him and Schapper triumphantly defend the entrance to a hall against hundreds of assailants!—a man no less energetic and resolute than his two comrades, but outstripping them in intelligence. Not only was he a born diplomat, as the success of his innumerable missions amply testifies; he also had a mind better fitted for theoretical issues. I made the acquaintance of all three in London during 1843. They were the first revolutionary proletarians I had met, and although our outlooks in those days differed on specific points—for what they had in the way of narrow-minded egalitarian communism*

---

* By egalitarian communism I mean that type of communism which is exclusively or mainly founded upon the demand for equality.

was amply compensated in me by a no less narrow-minded philosophical arrogance—I shall never forget the profound impression these three true men made upon me, a youngster at the time, just wanting to become a man.

In London, as to a lesser degree in Switzerland, the freedom of association and of assembly was of great advantage to them. Already on February 7, 1840, the German Workers Educational Society was founded, functioning not in secret but in the open. It still exists. The society served as a recruiting ground for the League and, since the communists were, as always, the most active and intelligent members of the Society, they took it as a matter of course that the leadership of the Society should be in the hands of the League. Very soon the League had several sections [*Gemeinden,* communes], or as they were still called at the time "huts" [*Hütten*], in London. In Switzerland and elsewhere these same tactics were followed. Wherever workers' societies could be formed they were made use of in the same way. Where legal prohibitions prevented such methods use was made of choral societies, sport societies, *Turnvereine,* and the like. Communications were kept up mainly by a continuous flow of traveling members going to and fro among the groups. Where necessary, these members also functioned as emissaries. In either case the activity of the League was greatly furthered by the governments of the day, which in their wisdom, by exiling every workman who had earned their disfavor—and in nine cases out of ten such a worker was a League member—converted him into an emissary.

The reconstructed League grew apace. In Switzerland this growth was particularly noticeable. Here Weitling, August Becker (an extremely gifted man, but who came to grief because of his temperamental instability, like so many Germans),[7] and others had formed a strong organization whose principles were more or less based on Weitling's communist system. This is not the place to criticize Weitling's communism. But, in order to show its importance as the first independent theoretical stirring of the German proletariat I still subscribe to Marx's words in the Paris *Vorwärts* of 1844: "Where could the German bourgeoisie, including its philosophers and divines, point to a work *championing bourgeois emancipation*—political emancipation—which can compare with Weitling's *Guaranties of Harmony and Freedom?* One who compares the jejune and faint-hearted mediocrity of German political literature with this tremendous and brilliant debut of the German workers, one who compares the *gigantic baby shoes of the proletariat* with the dwarfed and down-at-heel political shoes of the bourgeoisie, cannot but prophesy that Cinderella will grow to athletic stature." This athletic stature stands before us today although it still needs many years to grow to full proportions.

Many sections also existed in Germany, by their very nature perishable, but those that perished were replaced by new ones outnumbering the losses. Not until the end of 1846, seven years after the first groups had come into existence, did the German police discover in Berlin (Mentel) and Magdeburg (Beck) vestiges of the League, but were unable to follow up their discoveries.[8]

Before leaving Paris and going to Switzerland, Weitling, during 1840, had gathered the scattered elements of the League together again.

The nucleus of the League was composed of tailors. German tailors were everywhere, in Switzerland, in London, in Paris. In the last city German was so much the speech of the trade that in 1846 I knew a Norwegian tailor who had journeyed by sea from Drontheim to France, and during eighteen months had hardly learned a word of French. However, he had learned to speak an excellent German. Of the sections of the League in Paris existing in 1847, two were mainly composed of tailors, and one of cabinet makers.

No sooner was the center of gravity transferred from Paris to London than a new phenomenon came to the fore. The League, from being a German organization, gradually became an *international* one. In the Workers Educational Society one could find, in addition to Germans and Swiss, persons of other nationalities to whom the German language could serve as a medium of communication: there were Scandinavians, Dutch, Hungarians, Czechs,

Southern Slavs, also Russians and Alsatians. In 1847 a British grenadier of the guards, in uniform, was a regular attendant at the meetings. Soon the Society was called *Communist* Workers Educational Society. On the membership cards was found the slogan, "All Men Are Brothers," in at least twenty languages, although not always faultlessly. Just like the open Society, the secret League soon also began to assume a more international character. At first this international aspect was still limited in scope; it was in practice forced upon the League by the different nationalities of its members, and in theory by the realization that, for the revolution to be victorious, it needs must take place on a European scale. Beyond this the League did not go, but the foundations were laid.

Those who had fought in the insurrection of May 12, 1839, and had sought refuge in London, served as a link between the London League and the French revolutionists. The same held in the case of the more radical Poles. The official Polish refugees, as well as Mazzini, were of course more hostile than friendly. The English Chartists, because of the specifically English nature of their movement, were ignored as unrevolutionary. With these Chartists the leaders of the League in London came only in touch at a later date, through my intervention.

Circumstances led to yet other alterations in the character of the League. As was meet in those days, Paris was still looked upon as the revolutionary mother city. But the League had now begun to cut loose from the Parisian conspirators. Growing in size it grew in self-consciousness. Its members did come to feel that the League became more and more rooted in the German working class, and that these German workers were destined to be the standard bearers of the workers of Northern and Eastern Europe as a whole. The League had in Weitling a communist theoretician, who could rank with his French rivals as an equal. Moreover, the experience of May 12 had taught the lesson that the policy of attempted *Putsche* had become useless. Although every event was still looked upon as the possible starting point of a revolutionary outbreak, although the old, semi-conspiratorial rules were kept in their integrity, this was no more than a remnant of the ancient revolutionary obstinacy, already colliding with wiser and better outlooks.

We must state at the same time that the social doctrine of the League, in so far as it existed, was affected with a great error. This was due to the conditions of the time. The proletarian part of the membership consisted almost entirely of craftsmen. They were exploited by men who, even in the greatest cities, were nearly always themselves small masters. The exploitation of large-scale tailoring, so-called "confection," which occurred when the work was transformed into domestic industry in behalf of a great capitalist, was still in its infancy, even in London. The exploiter was himself a small master, and the workers in the trade lived in hope of becoming small masters themselves. In addition, vestiges of the guild spirit still adhered to the German craftsmen of these days. They were not as yet fully fledged modern proletarians, were only on the way to this status, were still hangers-on of the small middle class and had not at that date become the direct opponents of the bourgeoisie, that is, of large-scale capital. It serves these craftsmen to their greatest honor that they instinctively foresaw the future development of their class, and, though not fully conscious of the fact, were pressing forward toward organizing themselves as the party of the proletariat. Yet it was impossible to expect that their ingrained craft prejudices should not occasionally trip them up as soon as it came to a detailed criticism of existing society, that is to say, to an investigation of economic facts. I do not believe that one single member of the League had ever read a book on political economy. No matter! For the time being, "Equality," "Brotherhood," "Justice" gave them a leg over every theoretical stile.

In the meantime a new and essentially different kind of communism had been emerging alongside the communism of the League and of Weitling. While living in Manchester it was put right under my nose that economic facts, which so far have played no role or a despised one in the writing of history, are at least in the modern world a decisive historical force. They form the basis for the origin of present-day class antagonisms, and those antagonisms are—in those countries where, due to the existence of large-scale industry, they have been fully developed (as in England) —in turn the basis for the formation of political parties and their struggles and hence of all political history. Marx had not only come to the same conclusion, but already in 1844, writing in the *Deutsch-Französische Jahrbücher,* had generalized them to the effect that it is not the state which conditions and regulates bourgeois society, but bourgeois society which conditions and regulates the state—that, therefore, politics and its history have to be explained from the economic conditions and their evolution, not the other way about. When I visited Marx in Paris during the summer of 1844, it was obvious that we were in complete harmony as far as theoretical matters were concerned. From that time our working partnership can be dated. When in the spring of 1845 we met again, this time in Brussels, Marx had already advanced from these principles to the main aspects of his materialist theory of history. Now we set about the task of elaborating the newly gained theory in the most different directions.

The discovery of this theory, destined to revolutionize the science of history, is therefore in its essence the work of Marx, while I played in this matter only a very insignificant role. But the discovery was of immediate importance for the contemporary labor movement. Communism, among the French and the Germans, Chartism among the Britishers, now no longer appeared as chance phenomena which might just as well not have appeared at all. These were now seen as a movement of the modern suppressed class, the proletariat, they appeared as more or less developed forms of a historically necessary struggle against the ruling class, the bourgeoisie. They appeared as forms of class struggle, but different from earlier class struggles in the following particular: the oppressed class today, the proletariat, cannot achieve its own emancipation without liberating the whole of society from class divisions and with it from class struggles. And communism no longer signified an attempt to use your phantasy in order to concoct an ideal society as nearly perfect as possible. Communism meant henceforward understanding of the nature, the condition and the resulting general aims of the struggle conducted by the proletariat.

We had no wish to propound these new scientific results in ponderous tomes exclusively for the edification of the "learned" world. Quite the contrary. We had both of us entered bag and baggage into the political movement, we had certain followers in the educated world, especially in West Germany, and had close ties with the organized proletariat. In duty bound, we had to place our outlook upon a firm scientific foundation; but it was no less incumbent upon us to win the European proletariat in general and the German proletariat in particular over to our convictions. No sooner had we made the matter clear to ourselves than we set to work. We founded the German Workers Society at Brussels, and took possession of the *Deutsche Brüsseler Zeitung,* which served as our organ until the February revolution. We were in touch with the revolutionary section of English Chartists through Julian Harney,[9] the editor of *The Northern Star,* the central organ of the Chartists, to which I was a contributor. We also collaborated with the Brussels democrats (Marx was vice president of the Democratic Society),[10] and the French social democrats of *La Réforme,* to which I sent items concerning the English and the German movement. In a word, our relations with the radical and proletarian organizations and journals were as well as we could wish.

Our relations with the League of the Just were as follows. Of course we knew of the existence of this body: Schapper had invited me to become a member as long ago as 1843. For obvious reasons I had refused this invitation. Nevertheless we kept up a continuous correspondence with these Londoners, and were even more closely associated with Dr. Everbeck, then the leading figure of the Paris sections of the League.[11] Without troubling ourselves with the internal situation of the League we were nevertheless kept informed as to every important issue. By word of mouth, by letters, through newspaper articles we pressed our ideas upon the theoretical outlook of the most important members of the League. In addition we issued lithographed circulars on special occasions, where it concerned the internal affairs of the communist party now in formation, and sent them to our friends and correspondents wherever they were.[12] On occasion the League itself was made the issue.

This was the case with a young student from Westphalia [W. Germany], Herman Kriege, who had gone to America, where he gave himself out to be an emissary of the League. He associated with the madcap Harro Harring[13] to use the League in order to tear apart South America. He also founded a newspaper in which he expounded, in the name of the League, an extravagantly romanticizing communism overflowing with love [*Liebesduselei*]. We sallied forth to the attack by means of a circular which did not fail of its effect. As far as the League was concerned, Kriege was heard no more.

Later Weitling came to Brussels. But he was no longer the simple-hearted young journeyman tailor, who, rather awed by his own talents, had been eager to get a clear picture of just what a communist world would look like. He was now the great man persecuted by the envious because of his superiority, one who suspected rivals, secret enemies and snares everywhere; a prophet hounded from one country into another; a seer who had a recipe ready to hand for the realization of heaven upon earth and who fancied that everyone he encountered was trying to steal it from him. He had already become embroiled with the people of the London League. But in Brussels, where especially Marx and his wife had welcomed him with well-nigh superhuman forbearance, he got again into trouble with everyone. He therefore left soon for America hoping that there he would be able to continue his prophetic mission.

All these circumstances contributed to the quiet transformation which occurred in the League and particularly among the London leaders. The inadequacy both of French simplistic egalitarian communism and of Weitling's brand became to them clearer day by day. Weitling's endeavor to bring back communism to early Christian practice—and in his *Gospel of the Poor Sinner* there are luminous suggestions to this effect—had, in Switzerland, either thrown the movement into the hands of a fool like Albrecht or condemned it to exploitation by bogus prophets like Kuhlmann.[14] Then there was "true socialism," the affectation of a few belletristic souls, but it was no more than a translation of French socialist phrases into a corrupted Hegelian German, sickled over with sentimental effusions about love (see the section of the *Manifesto* on this type of socialism). Introduced into the League by Kriege and the readers of this kind of literature, its slobbing spinelessnes could only disgust the veteran revolutionists of the League. The theoretical ideas they hitherto held were obviously becoming untenable and the practical errors arising out of them became more and more apparent. Consequently those in London were increasingly convinced that Marx and I with our new theory were correct. The growth of this understanding was undoubtedly promoted by two men who happened to be members of the London League at the time, two men who far outstripped the other leaders in theoretical competence. They were Karl Pfänder, a miniature painter from Heilbronn, and Georg Eccarius, a tailor from Thüringen.[15] Pfänder died in London about eight years ago. He was a man of fine intelligence, original, witty, ironical, dialectical. Eccarius acted, as is well known, for many years as secretary of the International Working Men's Association, on whose General Council we find such names as Eccarius, Pfänder, Lessner, Lochner, Marx and my own. Subsequently Eccarius devoted himself entirely to the English trade union movement.

To cut a long story short, Moll came to Brussels in the spring of 1847. He visited Marx, and then came on to Paris to see me. His mission was to invite us once more, at the request of his comrades, to enter the League. They were convinced of the general correctness of our views, and no less convinced that the time had come for ridding the League of its traditional forms and conspirational methods. Should we enter the League, we should be given the opportunity, at a congress, to develop our critical communism in the shape of a manifesto to be published as the manifesto of the League. We should also be able to contribute to the replacement of the antiquated organization of the League by a new one in keeping with the times and with our aims.

We were in no doubt as to the need of an organization inside the German working class, if only for the sake of propaganda, nor did we fail to realize that such an organization, in so far as it was not of a purely local character, would have to be a secret one even outside of Germany. But such an organization already existed in the shape of the League. What we had hitherto been criticizing in this League was now recognized by the representatives of the League themselves as erroneous, we ourselves were asked to collaborate in the work of reorganization. Could we refuse? Certainly not. We therefore entered the League; Marx was able to found in Brussels a section from among our closer friends. For my part, I visited the three sections in Paris.

The first congress of the League took place in London during the summer of 1847. Wilhelm Wolff was the delegate of the Brussels section, I represented the Paris sections. The main theme was the reorganization of the League. Every vestige of the old mystical names, the heritage of conspiratorial days, was also discarded. The League was organized into sections [*Gemeinden*], circles, leading circles, central committee and congress. It took the name of Communist League. The first article of the new statutes was: "The aim of the League is the overthrow of the bourgeoisie, the domination of the proletariat, the abolition of the old bourgeois society based on class antagonisms, and the establishment of a new society without classes and without private property. . . ."[16]

The organization was democratic throughout; its officials were elected and subject to recall. This alone was sufficient to put an end to any hankering to revert to conspiratorial methods, for these require dictatorship, and the League was transformed—at least for ordinary times of peace—into a pure propaganda society. These new statutes—so democratic had we all become— were laid before the sections for discussion. They were further considered at the second congress, and were finally accepted by the body on December 8, 1847. They can be found in the book by Wermuth and Stieber, 1, p. 239, appendix VIII.[17]

The second congress took place during the last days of November and the early days of December of the same year. This time Marx was present and explained the new theory in the course of a lengthy debate—the congress lasted at least ten days. All opposition and doubt were at least set at rest, the new principles were unanimously accepted and Marx and I were commissioned to draw up the manifesto. We completed our task without delay. A few weeks before the outbreak of the February revolution, the manuscript was sent to London where it was printed.

Since that time it has made the voyage around the world, has been translated into almost every language and to this day serves as a guide to the proletarian movement. The motto of the old League: "All Men Are Brothers" was replaced by the new call to battle: "Proletarians of all Countries, Unite!" This was a public declaration of the international character of the struggle. Seventeen years later this call to battle resounded throughout the world as the war cry of the International Working Men's Association, and today the militant proletariat of all countries has inscribed it on its banner.

[*Engels continues with the history of the League during the revolutionary period 1848–49, which led to the anti-communist trial of 1852 in Cologne. For his complete account, see Marx and Engels,* Selected Works *(Int. Publ., New York, 1968) pp. 446–454.*]

II. THE COMMUNIST CREDOS
BY ENGELS

Engels wrote two "confessions of faith" or credos for the Communist League, one in June and the other in October 1847. The latter, which is known as "Principles of Communism," was consulted by Marx when he wrote the *Communist Manifesto.* The earlier document, "Draft of the Communist Confession of Faith," was found only in 1968.[1] The October document was first published in 1914.[2]

At the June 1847 Congress of the League of the Just, which was also the founding congress of the Communist League, it was decided to issue a draft "confession of faith" to be submitted for discussion to the sections of the League. The document which has now come to light is almost certainly this draft. It is lithographed in Engels' handwriting with the exception of the closing lines, beginning "In the name . . ." which are in the handwriting of Wolff and Schapper. That it was written by Engels also follows from the fact that at many places the text is identical with "Principles of Communism." In the latter, Engels left several questions unanswered, with the notation "stays" *(bleibt);* this clearly refers to the answers provided in the earlier draft.

Comparisons between the two documents show some differences in emphasis, reflecting not so much a change in Engels' outlook as a change in the outlook of the delegates between the first and the second congresses of the League. We know that at both congresses and in the period between them sharp debates on the principles of communism took place. The occasional vagueness in the first draft (e.g., "each human being is in search of happiness," Question 5) has disappeared in the second document, which is more concrete. Here Engels, probably in response to sharp questioning at the meetings of the League, goes rather deeply into what he believes can be said about a communist society without indulging in utopianism.

The early draft is presented here in our own English translation. Care has been taken that phrases identical in the October and June drafts are rendered by identical English phrases in the translation.

1.

DRAFT OF THE COMMUNIST CONFESSION OF FAITH

by F. Engels (June 1847)

QUESTION 1: *Are you a communist?*
Answer: Yes.
QUESTION 2: *What is the aim of the communists?*
To organize society in such a way that each of its members can develop and utilize all his potentialities and powers in full freedom without jeopardizing the foundations of this society.
QUESTION 3: *How do you plan to achieve this goal?*
By abolishing private property, replacing it by the community of goods.
QUESTION 4: *On what do you base your community of goods?*
Firstly, on the mass of productive powers and means of existence (*Lebensmittel*) generated by the development of industry, agriculture, trade and colonization, and on the possibility to increase them infinitely by machinery, chemical and other means.
Secondly, on the fact that in the consciousness or feeling of every human being there exist certain tenets as indisputable principles, tenets which, being the result of the whole historical development, are not in need of proof.
QUESTION 5: *Name some of those tenets.*
For instance, each human being is in search of happiness. The happiness of the individual is inseparably linked to the happiness of all, etc.

QUESTION 6: *How do you prepare for your community of goods?*

By enlightening and uniting the proletariat.

QUESTION 7: *What is the proletariat?*

The proletariat is that class of society which lives exclusively from its labor and not from the profit derived from capital; whose weal and woe, whose life and death depends on the alternation of good times and bad, in a word, on the vagaries of competition.

QUESTION 8: *Proletarians, then, have not always existed?*

No. Poor folk and working classes have always existed. The workers have also almost always been poor. But the proletarians have not always existed, any more than competition has always been free.

QUESTION 9: *How did the proletariat originate?*

The proletariat came into being with the introduction of machines invented since the middle of the last century, the most important being the steam engine, the spinning machine and the power loom. These machines were expensive and, consequently, could be installed only by rich persons. Their introduction displaced the workers of that time. This was due to the fact that machinery could produce more cheaply and rapidly than could the existing workers with their imperfect spinning wheels and hand looms. The machines thus handed industry over entirely to the big capitalists and rendered the scant property the workers possessed and which mainly consisted of their tools, hand looms, etc., entirely worthless. The capitalists got all in their hands and nothing remained for the workers. Thus the factory system was introduced.

When the capitalists realized how advantageous this was to them, they tried to extend it to more and more branches of industry. They divided the work more and more between the workers, so that in the course of time the worker who had been wont to make the entire article now only made a part. Such simplified work delivered the products quicker and therefore cheaper and it was now found that in almost every branch of industry machinery could also be applied.

As soon as a branch of industry could be mechanized, it fell, like spinning and weaving, into the hands of the big capitalists and the workers were deprived of their last shred of independence. Gradually it has come about that almost every branch of industry has fallen under the sway of the factory system. The present middle class, especially the small master handicraftsmen, have been slowly driven to ruin; the workers have had their existence completely transformed, and new classes have come into being, absorbing all other classes of society. They are:

I. The class of big capitalists, who in all civilized countries are now almost exclusive owners of means of subsistence and of such means (machines, factories, workshops, etc.) needed for the production of these means of subsistence. This is the class of the *bourgeois* or the *bourgeoisie.*

II. The class of the totally dispossessed, who are compelled to sell their labor to the bourgeois in order to provide their means of subsistence. Since the parties to this trade in labor are *not* on equal terms, the bourgeois having the advantage, the dispossessed must yield of necessity to the bad conditions offered by the bourgeois. This class dependent on the bourgeois is called the class of proletarians or the *proletariat.*

QUESTION 10: *In what way does the proletarian differ from the slave?*

The slave is sold once and for all. The proletarian must sell himself by the day and by the hour. The slave is the property of a master and precisely because of this has his existence assured, be that existence ever so wretched. The proletarian is as it were the slave of the whole bourgeois *class,* not of one single master, and thus has no assured existence, since nobody buys his labor unless he needs it. The slave is counted an *object* and not a member of civil society. The proletarian is recognized as a *person,* as a member of civil society. The slave may therefore be able to secure better conditions of life than can the proletarian, but the proletarian belongs to a higher stage of development. The slave frees himself by becoming a *proletarian* and by rupturing, of all relations of private property, only the relation of slavery. The proletarian can only achieve emancipation by abolishing private property in its entirety.

QUESTION 11: *In what way does the proletarian differ from the serf?*

The serf utilizes a strip of land, hence an instrument of production, in exchange for a larger or a smaller portion of the yield. The proletarian works with instruments of production which are the property of somebody else, who reimburses him with a certain portion of the product determined by the competition. The portion of the worker is determined by his own labor, hence by himself in the case of the serf. In the case of the proletarian it is determined by competition, hence primarily by the bourgeois. The serf has security of existence, the proletarian has no such security. The serf can gain his liberty by throwing off his feudal lord and become a property owner himself, hence entering the realm of competition and joining for the time being the possessing class, the privileged class. The proletarian frees himself by abolishing property, competition and all class distinctions.

QUESTION 12: *In what way does the proletarian differ from the artisan?*

In contrast to the proletarian, the so-called artisan, as he still existed almost everywhere in the past century and still exists here and there at present, is a proletarian at most *temporarily*. He has the intent to acquire capital himself wherewith to exploit other workers. He can often achieve this goal where guilds still exist or where freedom from guild restrictions has not yet led to the introduction of factory-style methods into the crafts and has not led to fierce competition. But as soon as the factory system has been introduced into the crafts and competition flourishes fully, this perspective dwindles away and the artisan becomes more and more a proletarian. The artisan therefore frees himself by becoming either bourgeois or entering the middle class in general, or becoming a proletarian because of competition (as is now more often the case). In that case he can free himself by joining the proletarian movement, i.e. the more or less conscious communist movement.

QUESTION 13: *You therefore do not believe that the community of goods was possible at all times?*

No. Communism has only appeared since machines and other inventions made it possible to offer to all members of society the promise of an all-around education, a happy existence. Communism is the doctrine of a liberation not open to the slave, the serf or the artisan, but for the first time to the proletarian. It therefore belongs necessarily to the 19th century and was not possible at an earlier date.

QUESTION 14: *Let us return to the sixth question. When you wish to prepare the community by enlightening and unifying the proletariat, do you therefore reject the revolution?*

We are convinced not only of the futility, but even of the harmfulness of all conspiracies. We also know that revolutions are not made deliberately and at will, but that everywhere and at all times revolutions are the necessary outcome of circumstances quite independent of the will and guidance of particular parties and whole classes. But along with this we perceive that the development of the proletariat is in nearly all countries of the world violently suppressed by the possessing classes and that by this method the opponents of communism are working might and main toward a revolution. If these methods would at long last drive the oppressed proletariat into a revolution, then we will rally to the cause of the workers and be just as prompt to act as we are now to speak.

QUESTION 15: *Do you wish to replace the social order of today all at once by the community of goods?*

By no means. You cannot decree the development of the masses. This is conditioned by the development of the conditions in which these masses live and hence evolve gradually.

QUESTION 16: *In what way do you believe that the transition from the present condition to the community of goods can be accomplished?*

The first basic condition for the introduction of the community of goods is the political liberation of the proletariat by a democratic state of society [*Staatsverfassung*].

QUESTION 17: *What will be your first measure as soon as you have established democracy?*

Guaranteeing the proletariat the means for its existence.

QUESTION 18: *How are you going to carry this out?*

I. By such restriction of private property that prepares its gradual conversion into communal property, e.g., by progressive taxation, restriction of the right of inheritance in favor of the state, etc.

II. By the employment of the workers in national workshops and factories, as well as on the national domain.

III. By the education of all children at the expense of the state.

QUESTION 19: *How will you organize this education in the transition period?*

All children will be educated and instructed in state institutions from the moment they are old enough to dispense with the first maternal care.

QUESTION 20: *Will the community of women not be proclaimed at the same time as the community of goods?*

Not at all. We shall interfere with the private relationship between husband and wife, and the family in general, only in so far as the new order of society would be hampered by the preservation of the existing forms. Moreover, we know very well that in the course of history the family relationship has experienced modifications in accordance with the different property relationships and periods of development. The abolition of private property will therefore also substantially affect this family relationship.

QUESTION 21: *Will nationalities continue under communism?*

The nationalities of the peoples associating themselves in accordance with the principle of community will be compelled to mingle with each other as a result of this association. In this way they will have to dissolve themselves, just as the various estate and class distinctions must disappear through the abolition of their basis, private property.

QUESTION 22: *Do the communists reject existing religions?*

All religions so far have been the expression of historical stages of development of individual peoples or masses of people. But communism is that stage of historical development which makes all existing religions superfluous and brings about their disappearance [*aufhebt*].

In the name and by mandate of the congress:

The secretary   *The chairman*

HEIDE.   CARL SCHILL[3]

London, June 9, 1847

2.

PRINCIPLES OF COMMUNISM

by F. Engels (October 1847)

QUESTION 1: *What is communism?*

Answer: Communism is the doctrine of the prerequisites for the emancipation of the proletariat.

QUESTION 2: *What is the proletariat?*

Answer: The proletariat is that class of society whose means of livelihood entirely depend on the sale of its labor and not on the profit derived from capital; whose weal and woe, whose life and death, whose whole existence depend on the demand for labor, hence on the alternation of good times and bad, on the vagaries of unbridled competition. The proletariat, or class of proletarians, is, in a word, the working class of the 19th century.

QUESTION 3: *Proletarians, then, have not always existed?*

Answer: No. Poor folk and working classes have always existed. The working classes have also for the most part been poor. But such poor, such workers as are living under conditions indicated above, hence proletarians, have not always existed, any more than free and unbridled competition has always existed.

QUESTION 4: *How did the proletariat originate?*

Answer: The proletariat originated in the industrial revolution which took place in England during the second half of the 18th century and which has repeated itself since then in all the civilized countries of the world. This industrial revolution took place owing to the invention of the steam engine, of various spinning machines, of the power loom, and of a great number of other mechanical instruments. These machines were expensive and, consequently, could only be installed by persons who had plenty of capital to lay out. Their introduction completely altered the existing method of production and displaced the existing workers. This was due to the fact that machinery could produce cheaper and better commodities than could the handicraftsmen with their imperfect spinning wheels and hand looms. Thus, these machines handed over industry entirely to the big capitalists and rendered the little property the workers possessed (tools, hand looms, etc.) entirely worthless. Soon the capitalists got all in their hands and nothing remained for the workers. Thus it was that in the realm of textile production the factory system was first introduced.

The impetus once having been given, machinery and the factory system rapidly invaded all the other branches of production. The first to succumb were the cloth and book-printing trades, pottery, and metalware industry. More and more did the various processes come to be divided among individual workers, so that in the course of time the worker who had been wont to make the entire article with his own hands, now merely produced a part of the article. This division of labor made production speedier and the commodities could be sold cheaper. The labor of each worker was simplified immensely, his movements were reduced to a mechanical action repeated time after time, which the machine not only could perform just as well, but a good deal better. Gradually all industries fell under the dominance of steam power, of machinery, and of the factory system; all alike followed in the footsteps of the spinning and weaving industries. In this way they came totally into the hands of the big capitalists, and the workers were also here deprived of their last shred of independence. In addition to genuine manufacture, handicrafts likewise came to be absorbed into the factory system. Here also the big owners of capital were able to lay out money on the erection of huge workshops, whereby much expense was spared and the labor here also could be divided among the workers. Gradually the small masters were squeezed out. This is the process by which in the civilized countries almost every branch of industry has fallen under the sway of the factory system, the process which has ousted handicraft and manufacture in favor of large-scale production. —The present middle class, especially the small master craftsmen, have thus been slowly driven to ruin; the workers have had their existence completely transformed; and two new classes have come into being, absorbing all other classes of society. They are:

I. The class of the big capitalists, who in all civilized countries are now almost exclusive owners of the means of subsistence and the raw materials and instruments (machinery, factories, etc.), needed for the production of these means of subsistence. This is the class of the bourgeois or the bourgeoisie.

II. The class of the totally dispossessed, who are compelled to sell their labor to the bourgeois in order to provide the necessary means of subsistence for themselves and their families. This class is called the class of the proletarians or the proletariat.

QUESTION 5: *Under what conditions does the sale of labor of proletarians to the bourgeoisie take place?*

Answer: Labor is a commodity like any other commodity and its price is determined according to the same laws as those which govern the price of other commodities. The price of a commodity under the dominion of large-scale industry or of free competition (the two, as we shall see, amount to the same thing) is on the average always equal to the cost of production of this commodity. The price of labor is, therefore, likewise equivalent to its cost of production. But the cost of production of labor consists of that sum of the means of subsistence which is necessary to keep the worker fit to perform the labor and to prevent the working class from dying out. Thus the worker will not receive more for his labor than is sufficient for this purpose. The price of labor, or wages, is therefore the minimum, the lowest amount at which the life of the worker can be maintained. Since business is subject to ups and downs, the worker will receive now more, now less, just as the factory owner receives now more, now less for his commodities. But just as the factory owner receives on the average, be the times good or be they bad, neither more nor less for his commodities than the cost of their production, so does the worker, on the average, receive neither more nor less than this minimum. This economic law of the wages of labor will come to be the more stringently applied, the more all branches of industry are absorbed by large-scale processes of production.*

QUESTION 6: *Which working classes existed before the industrial revolution?*

Answer: The living conditions of the working classes have varied in accordance with the different stages of development of society; the relations of the working classes to the possessing and ruling classes have altered in like manner. In the days of Antiquity the workers were the *slaves* of those who owned them, just as they even still exist in backward lands and even in the southern part of the United States. During the Middle Ages the workers were *serfs* belonging to the lords of the soil; these relations still exist in Hungary, Poland, and Russia. In addition to serfs, there were in those medieval days in the towns, until the Industrial Revolution, handicraftsmen of various sorts in the service of petty bourgeois masters. Gradually, with the development of manufacture, manufacturing workers appeared already employed by bigger capitalists.

QUESTION 7: *In what way does the proletarian differ from the slave?*

Answer: The slave is sold once and for all. The proletarian must sell himself by the hour or by the day. Each individual slave, being the direct property of a master, has his existence assured, be that existence ever so wretched, if only because of the interest of the slave owner. Each individual proletarian, the property as it were of the whole bourgeois *class,* whose labor is sold only when it is needed by the owning class, has no security of life. Existence is merely guaranteed to the working *class* as a whole. The slave is excluded from competition; the proletarian is beset by competition and is a prey to all its fluctuations. The

---

* This pre-Marxist view of labor (rather than labor power) as a commodity was later rejected by Marx and Engels as Marx developed the theory of surplus value (*see, Capital* I, Part VI, "Wages"; and Marx, *Wage-Labour and Capital,* as edited by Engels.—*Ed.*

slave is counted an object and not a member of civil society; the proletarian is recognized as a person, as a member of civil society. The slave may therefore be able to secure better conditions of life than can the proletarian, but the proletarian belongs to a higher stage of development of society than the slave. The slave frees himself by rupturing, of all relations of private ownership, only one, the relation of slavery and by this act becomes himself a proletarian; the proletarian can only achieve emancipation by abolishing private property in its entirety.

QUESTION 8: *In what way does the proletarian differ from the serf?*

Answer: The serf owns and utilizes an instrument of production, a strip of land; in exchange he hands over a portion of the yield or he gives a certain amount of labor to his lord. The proletarian works with instruments of production which belong to another than himself, he labors for the other and receives a portion of the product in return. The serf gives; the proletarian receives. Security of existence is granted to the serf but not to the proletarian. The serf is not enmeshed in the competitive struggle; the proletarian is. The serf can gain his liberty by running away to the town and there becoming a handicraftsman; or he may pay his lord in money instead of in kind, thereby becoming a free tenant; or he may throw off his feudal lord and become a property owner himself, in a word, he may by a variety of methods enter the ranks of the possessing class and enter the circle of competition. The proletarian frees himself by abolishing competition, private property and all class distinctions.

QUESTION 9: *In what way does the proletarian differ from the artisan?*

Answer: [The answer is lacking.][4]

QUESTION 10: *What is the difference between the proletarian and the worker in manufacture?*

Answer: The manufacturing period proper lasted from the 16th to the 18th century and during this time the worker owned almost everywhere an instrument of production, his loom, the family spinning wheels, and his little plot of land which he cultivated in his leisure hours. The proletarian has none of these things. The majority of manufacturing workers lived on the land under more or less patriarchal relations with his lord or his employer; the proletarian usually dwells in large towns and his relation to his employer is purely a money relation. The manufacturing worker is torn out of the patriarchal conditions of his life by big industry, loses all he has, and thereby becomes himself a proletarian.

QUESTION 11: *What were the first results of the industrial revolution and the division of society into bourgeois and proletarian?*

Answer: In the first place the old system of manufacture or industry dependent upon hand labor was totally destroyed by the products of machine industry, which could be put on the market at ever cheaper rates. All semi-barbarian countries, hitherto more or less inaccessible to the historical evolutionary process and whose industry had been based on these old manufacturing methods, were forcibly dragged out of their isolation by this development. They bought the cheaper commodities from England and allowed their own manufacturing workers to perish. Thus it was that countries which had stagnated for centuries, India for example, were revolutionized from top to base; even in China such a revolution is at hand. It has come to the point that within a year of the introduction of a new machine into an English factory, millions of workers in China are thrown out of work. Large-scale industry has thus brought all the peoples of the earth into relationships one with another, has thrown all small local markets together into one huge world market, has everywhere introduced civilization and progress, and has arranged matters in such a way that when anything happens in the civilized countries the events have their repercussion in all other lands. Were the workers of England and of France, for instance, to win their liberty today, this would cause revolutions to occur in other countries which in course of time would lead to the emancipation of all their workers.

Secondly, wherever large-scale industry has replaced manufacture, the bourgeoisie has developed its power and its wealth to the highest degree and has risen to the position of the dominant class in the country. Consequently, wherever this took place, the bourgeoisie seized political power, and the aristocracy and the guild burgesses who had hitherto been the ruling classes, together with the absolute monarchy which was their representative, were elbowed out of the way. The bourgeoisie destroyed the power of the landed aristocracy by abolishing entailed property and the privileges of the nobility. The bourgeoisie destroyed the power of the guild burgesses by destroying the guilds and craft privileges. Their place was taken by free competition, thus allowing every member of society the right to carry on any industry he fancies, without hindrance but for lack of the necessary capital. The introduction of free competition constitutes the public declaration that henceforward members of society are unequal only insofar as the capital they respectively own differs in quantity, that capital is the decisive power, and that, consequently, the capitalists, the bourgeois, have become the leading class in society. Free competition is necessary in the early days of large-scale industry, for it is the only social form in which this kind of industrial life can flourish. As soon as the bourgeoisie had destroyed the social power of the aristocrats and the guild burgesses, it proceeded to annihilate their political power as well. Having become the leading class in the social order, the bourgeoisie now also proclaimed itself the leading class in the political world. This was brought about by the introduction of the representative system of government which rests upon the bourgeois doctrine of equality before the law and the legal recognition of free competition. In European lands it has taken the form of constitutional monarchy. In these constitutional monarchies the voters are only those who possess a certain amount of capital; that is to say, the voters are only the bourgeois. These bourgeois voters elect the deputies, and the bourgeois deputies, having the right to refuse taxes, elect a bourgeois government.

Thirdly, the proletariat has grown everywhere in step with the bourgeoisie. In the same proportion as the bourgeoisie gains wealth, the proletariat gains in numbers. Since proletarians can be employed only where capital is available and since capital can increase only when it employs labor, the growth of the proletariat proceeds at the same pace as the growth of capital. Simultaneously, bourgeois as well as proletarians are drawn together in large cities, because here the conditions are most favorable for the carrying on of industry. This herding together of great masses of human beings in one area makes the proletarians conscious of their power. Furthermore, the more this process advances, the more new machines are introduced that drive out handicraft production, the more industry depresses wages to their minimum, and the proletariat's condition is rendered more and ever more unbearable. Thus, growing discontent on the part of the workers and their growing power prepare the way for a social revolution brought about by the proletariat.

QUESTION 12: *What have been the further consequences of the industrial revolution?*

Answer: By means of the steam engine and various other machines, large-scale industry had the means, in a short period of time and at slight expense, to increase production to an almost unlimited extent. Free competition, which is a necessary consequence of large-scale production, very soon assumed an extremely aggressive aspect, due to the ease with which commodities were produced. A number of capitalists hurled themselves into industrial life, and very soon more was produced than could be utilized. Consequently, machine-made wares could not be sold, and a so-called commercial crisis ensued. Factories had to be closed, factory owners went bankrupt, and the workers went without bread. Suffering was rife everywhere. After a while the surplus products were sold, the factory wheels were again set a-going, wages went up, and gradually business was more brisk than ever. But this prosperity did not last long. Again too many commodities were produced, another crisis ensued, and ran the same course as the previous one. During the whole of this century, industrial life has fluctuated between times of prosperity and times of crisis; and nearly every five to seven years a similar crisis has recurred, bringing in its train the intolerable wretchedness of the workers, a general revolutionary stirring, and exposing the extant order of society to the greatest dangers.

QUESTION 13: *What are the consequences of these regularly recurring commercial crises?*

Answer: First, although in its initial stages large-scale industry itself gave birth to free competition, now it has outgrown its own creation. Competition and in general the carrying on of industry by individual capitalists has become a fetter upon production, and this fetter must be shattered. Large-scale industry, so long as it is conducted as at present, can recover its prosperity only through a seven-yearly upheaval which is a menace to civilization, not merely casting the proletariat into a well of misery but likewise causing the ruin of a great number of bourgeois. Either large-scale industry must be abolished, which is quite out of the question, or it needs a totally different social order wherein to function. The new social order would no longer be led by individual factory owners competing one against the other, but industrial production would be led by the whole of society according to a settled plan and according to the needs of all the members of society.

Secondly, large-scale industry and the resulting limitless expansion of production makes it possible to inaugurate a social order wherein so many necessities of life are produced that every member of society will be able to develop and exercise all his energies and capacities in the fullest freedom. It thus appears that precisely those qualities of large-scale industry which now produce all misery and all crises will in another social order promote the abolition of such suffering and catastrophical trade fluctuations. Thus it is obvious that:

1. All those evils are from now on to be ascribed to a social order which is no longer compatible with the actual requirements of society.

2. The means are ready to hand for putting an end to these evils through a new social order.

QUESTION 14: *What form will this new social order assume?*

Answer: First of all, the running of industries and all branches of production will be taken out of the hands of individuals and competing individuals. All branches of production will be operated by society as a whole, this is to say that industry will be run according to a common account, according to a common plan and by the participation of all members of society. Competition therefore will be done away with, and association will take its place. Since the running of industry by individual capitalists inevitably presupposes the existence of private property, and since free competition is the outcome of the individual ownership of industrial concerns, private ownership cannot be separated from free competition and individually owned industrial concerns. Thus private ownership will also have to be abolished, and in its stead we shall have the utilization of all the instruments of production and the distribution of the products among all members of society by common agreement. In a word, we shall have what is called community of goods. The term "abolition of private property" is indeed the most succinct and significant way of formulating the change in the total social order rendered necessary by the development of industry. The communists are right, therefore, to place this in the forefront of their demands.

QUESTION 15: *Was the abolition of private property not possible at an earlier date?*

Answer: No. Every change in the social order, every revolution in property relations, is the necessary outcome of the creation of new productive forces which cannot fit properly into the old system of property relations. Private property itself came to birth in this way. For private property has not always existed. When toward the close of the Middle Ages a new method of production was introduced, the manufacturing system, this new system, having outgrown the feudalist and the guild property relations, created a new form of property, private property. No other property form than that of private property was possible during the period of manufacture and in the early stages of the development of large-scale industry; no other order of society was possible than that founded upon private property. There must always be a dominant class controlling the forces of production and a poverty-stricken, oppressed class, so long as there is not enough produced to supply not only the immediate wants of all the members of society, but also a surplus of products for the increase of social capital and for the further development of the forces of production. The way in which these classes are constituted will depend upon the stage of development which the productive system has reached. The Middle Ages were dependent upon agriculture, and, consequently, we find baron and serf; during the later Middle Ages, the towns provide us with the master guildsman and his apprentices and day laborers; the 17th century has manufacturers and workers in manufacture; the 19th century gave birth to the big factory owners and the proletarians. It is obvious that hitherto the productive forces had not been developed widely enough to provide enough for all members of society, and that private property had not yet become a fetter, a hindrance, to these productive forces. In our day, when the productive forces have attained so high a degree of development that, *firstly,* capitalists and productive forces are called into being on a scale hitherto unheard of and the means exist for multiplying these forces without limit; that, *secondly,* these productive forces are concentrated in the hands of a few bourgeois whilst the great mass of the people are falling into the ranks of the proletariat, the condition of the latter becoming more wretched and unendurable in proportion to the accumulation of wealth by the bourgeois; that, *thirdly,* these mighty and easily multiplied productive forces have so vastly outgrown the bourgeois and his private property that they constantly involve the social order in colossal disturbances—the abolition of private property is not only possible but even in the highest degree necessary.

QUESTION 16: *Will it be possible to bring about the abolition of private property by peaceful methods?*

Answer: This is greatly to be desired, and communists would be the last persons in the world to stand in the way of a peaceful solution. Communists know only too well the futility and, indeed, the harmfulness of conspiratorial methods. They know only too well that revolutions are not made deliberately and arbitrarily, but that everywhere and at all times revolutions have been the necessary outcome of circumstances quite independent of the will or the guidance of particular parties and whole classes. But they also perceive that the development of the proletariat in nearly all civilized countries is violently suppressed, and that in this way opponents of communism are working full force to promote a revolution. Should the oppressed proletariat at long last thus be driven into a revolution, then we communists will rally to the cause of the workers and be just as prompt to act as we are now to speak.

QUESTION 17: *Will it be possible to abolish private property all at once?*

Answer: No. This would be just as impossible as to multiply all at once the existing forces of production to the degree necessary for the inauguration of the community. The proletarian revolution, which in all probability is coming, will for this reason, only be able to transform present society gradually. Private property will be abolished only when the means of production have become available in sufficient quantities.

QUESTION 18: *What will be the course of the revolution?*

Answer: In the first place it will draw up a *democratic constitution* and by means of this establish directly or indirectly the political rule of the proletariat. In England, for instance, where the proletariat is in the majority, the rule of the proletariat will be direct. In France and in Germany, where the majority of the population consists, in addition to proletarians, of peasants producing on a small scale and of lower middle-class citizens, it will be indirect. For the two last-named categories are only now beginning to become proletarians, and their political interests are becoming more and more dependent on those of the proletariat, so that soon they must adapt themselves to the demands of the proletariat. Perhaps this will entail a second fight, but it will result inevitably in the victory of the proletariat.

Democracy would be of no use to the proletariat unless it should serve at once as the means for a direct attack upon private property and for the safeguarding of the livelihood of the proletariat. The main measures, which already now appear as the necessary results of the existing relationships, are the following:

1. Limitation of private ownership by means of progressive taxation, high death duties, abolition of inheritance by collateral lines (brothers, nephews, etc.) , forced loans, and so forth.

2. Gradual expropriation of landed proprietors, factory owners, railway owners and owners of shipping concerns *(Schiffsreeder)*, partly through competition by State industries and in part directly through payment of compensation in currency notes *(Assignaten)*.

3. Confiscation of the property of all émigrés and rebels against the majority of the people.

4. Organization of the labor or occupation of the proletariat on the national domains, in factories and workshops, thereby putting an end to competition among the workers themselves and forcing the remaining factory owners to pay the same high wages as those paid by the State.

5. An equal obligation to work for all members of society until the abolition of private property is completed. Organization of industrial armies, especially for agriculture.

6. Centralization of credit and finance in the hands of the State, by means of a national bank with State capital and the suppression of all private banks and bankers.

7. Increase of national factories, workshops, railways, and shipping, cultivation of uncultivated land and improvement of already cultivated land in proportion to the increase in capital and labor at the disposal of the nation.

8. Education of all children, as soon as they are old enough to dispense with maternal care, in national institutions and at the charge of the nation. Education and production together.

9. The erection of palatial dwellings on the national domains where communities of citizens shall live together for the carrying on of industry and agriculture; where the advantages of town life shall be linked with those of the country without the one-sidedness and the disadvantages of either.

10. The demolition of all unsanitary and badly built houses and urban quarters.

11. Equal right of inheritance for illegitimate as for legitimate children.

12. Concentration of all means of transportation in the hands of the nation.

Of course, we cannot expect all these measures to be introduced simultaneously. But the introduction of one will lead to the introduction of others. Once the initial radical onslaught upon private ownership has been made, the proletariat will find itself forced to go ever further, and more and more to concentrate in the hands of the State all capital, all agriculture, all industries, all transport facilities, and all means of exchange. That is the aim of all the above-mentioned measures, and they and their centralizing results will be realizable in the same proportion as the productive forces of the country are increased through the labor of the proletariat. Finally, when all capital, all production, and all exchange are concentrated in the hands of the nation, private ownership will have ceased to exist on its own account, money will have become superfluous, and production will have so increased and men will have so changed that the last vestiges of the old social relations will have disappeared.

QUESTION 19: *Can such a revolution take place in one country alone?*

Answer: No. Large-scale industry, by creating a world market, has so linked up the peoples of the earth, and especially the civilized peoples, that each of them is dependent on what happens in other lands. Further, the social development of all civilized countries has become so similar that everywhere the struggle between bourgeoisie and proletariat, the two classes of society upon which the issue depends, has become the dominating struggle of the day. The communist revolution will, therefore, not be a national revolution alone; it will take place in all civilized countries, or at least in England, America, France and Germany, at one and the same time. In each of these countries it will take a longer or a shorter time to develop according to whether one country or the other has a more developed industry, greater wealth, a more important quantity of productive forces at its disposal. The revolution will therefore assume its slowest pace and be most difficult of achievement in Germany; in England it will go ahead quickly and easily. It will exercise considerable influence upon all other countries of the world, totally changing and very much hastening the present process of their development. This is to be a universal revolution, and will, therefore, have a universal field for its operations.[5]

QUESTION 20: *What will be the consequences of the final abolition of private ownership?*

Answer: In this case society has deprived the capitalists of their private use of the forces of production, transport, exchange and distribution, and is able to administer all these in a planned way according to the need of society as a whole and according to the means at its command. Then, most important of all, the evil consequences now associated with big industry will be eliminated. Crises will cease to be; the increase of production, which in the present order of society spells over-production and is such a great cause of suffering, will then not even suffice to meet the need and will have to be greatly stimulated. Instead of bringing wretchedness in its wake, over-production beyond the immediate wants of society will satisfy the needs of all, and create new needs, and at the same time the means for their gratification. It will cause and stimulate further progress, it will achieve this progress without, as heretofore, thereby throwing society into confusion. Once liberated from the yoke of private ownership, large-scale industry will develop on a new scale that will dwarf the present machine industry as conspicuously as this has dwarfed the manufacturing system of earlier days. The growth of industry will provide a quantity of products sufficient to gratify the needs of all. The same will be true for agricultural production, hitherto cramped and hindered by the weight of private ownership and the excessive subdivision of farming land. Here scientific methods and improvements of all sorts will soon result in a totally new leap forward, which will provide amply for society's needs. Thus society will have at its disposal such a quantity of products that distribution among its members will be equitable and satisfactory. The division of society into various antagonistic classes will then become superfluous. Nay, more; not only will such class divisions be superfluous, they will be incompatible with the new social order. Classes came into existence through the division of labor; the division of labor, as hitherto known, will disappear entirely. Mechanical and chemical auxiliaries do not alone suffice to develop industrial and agricultural production to the level we have described. The faculties of the men who set these auxiliaries in motion must undergo a corresponding development. Just as the peasant and the worker in manufacture of the last century were forced to change the whole of their habits and customs, and even had to become totally different human beings when they were swept into the current of large-scale industry, so also, communal production by the whole of society and the resulting new development of production will need entirely different men, and, indeed, will also produce them. The men of today cannot be expected to adapt themselves to the methods involved in communal production, for now each individual is engaged in one branch of production to the exclusion of all others, is shackled and exploited by it; he can cultivate only one of his faculties at the cost of all others, knows only one branch, or, indeed, only a branch of a branch of production as a whole. Even contemporary industry finds such workers less and less useful. But when the whole of society shall carry on industry in common and according to plan, then men will be needed whose faculties have been developed from every point of view, men able to comprehend the entire system of production. The division of labor already undermined by the machine system, the division of labor which compels one man to be a peasant, another a cobbler, another a factory hand, another a stock market operator, will disappear completely. Education will teach the young folk to familiarize themselves quickly with the whole system of production, they will be in a position to pass from one branch of industry to another according to the needs of society or their own inclinations. They will no longer, as today, be one-sided in their development as a result of the division of labor. Thus a communistically organized society will be able to provide opportunities for the all-round cultivation of all-round faculties. Simultaneously with this development, social classes necessarily must vanish, for on the one hand classes cannot exist in a communist society, and, on the other, the very organization of this society provides the means of abolishing these class differences.

It follows from all this that the contrast between town and countryside will likewise disappear. The fact that agriculture and industrial production will be carried on by the same individuals rather than by two different classes of society, lies at the very foundation of communist association and is, if only for material reasons alone, an essential feature of such association. The dispersal of the agricultural population throughout the countryside, in contrast with the crowding of the industrial population in the towns, corresponds to the fact that both agriculture and industry have reached but a very low state of development. It constitutes an obstacle to future development, an obstacle that can be felt even now.

The general association of all members of society for the purpose of common and planned utilization of the productive forces, the expansion of production so that it suffices to provide for the needs of all, the cessation of that condition whereby the satisfaction of the needs of one is effected only at the cost of the needs of others, the complete destruction of classes and their antagonisms, the all-round development of the talents of all the members of society by means of the abolition of the hitherto prevalent division of labor by means of industrial education, the variation of activities, the participation of all in the enjoyments produced by all, the unification of town and countryside—such are the main results of the abolition of private ownership.[6]

QUESTION 21: *What influence will the communist order of society have upon the family?*

Answer: It will make the relations between the sexes a purely private affair, which concerns only the two persons involved; a relationship which is in no way the concern of society. This attitude is made possible because private property will have been abolished and the children will be educated communally. The two foundation stones of hitherto existing marriage, the dependence, based on private property, of the wife upon her husband and of the children upon the parents, thus will have been abolished. This is also the answer to the outcry made by highly moral philistines against the "communist community of women." Community of women is a relationship entirely peculiar to bourgeois society; it exists today in a complete form in prostitution. Prostitution is rooted in private ownership; destroy the latter and prostitution falls with it. Far from inaugurating an era of communal ownership of women, communistic organization of society in fact abolishes it.

QUESTION 22: *How will the communist regime deal with the existing nationalities?*

Stays [*bleibt*].

QUESTION 23: *How will it deal with the existing religions?*
Stays.[7]

QUESTION 24: *In what way are the communists different from the socialists?*

Answer: The so-called socialists may be divided into three groups.

The first group consists of adherents of feudal and patriarchal society, which has been or is being destroyed by the growth of large-scale industry, world trade, and the bourgeois society which these two have brought into existence. This group advocates the following remedy for the evils of present-day society: Re-establish the feudal and patriarchal order, for it was free of these evils. All their proposals lead directly or indirectly to this goal. This group of *reactionary* socialists, despite apparent sympathy and hot tears for the miseries of the proletariat, must always be opposed strenuously by the communists, for the following reasons:

1. It is striving after the impossible.

2. It endeavors to re-establish the rule of the aristocracy, the guild masters and the manufacturers, with their retinue of absolute or feudal monarchs, officials, soldiery and priests; a society which was free, it is true, from present-day evils, but which nevertheless had at the least quite as many evils of its own; a society, moreover, offering no hopes for the liberation of the oppressed workers by a communist organization.

3. It reveals its genuine sentiments whenever the proletariat turns revolutionary and communistic, in which case it immediately rallies to the side of the bourgeoisie against the proletarians.

The second group is composed of adherents of our contemporary social order, of people who are anxious lest the evils which are the inevitable outcome of the present social order should bring this society down to destruction. They are, therefore, endeavoring to maintain the present social order while at the same time eliminating the evils arising from it. With this end in view, some of them propose various welfare regulations, while others among them advocate grandiose reform systems, which, under pretext of reorganizing society, are in fact intended to retain the foundations of the present-day social order, and hence to retain the present state of things intact. These *bourgeois socialists* likewise will have to be opposed persistently by the communists, for they work for the foes of communism and defend that very social order which the communists are out to overthrow.

Finally, the third group is made up of democratic socialists. These accept some of the measures advocated by the communists in the answer to Question 18, but not as measures for the period of transition to communism, but as measures sufficient for the abolition of misery and the other evils of existing society. These *democratic socialists* are either proletarians who are not yet awake to the conditions necessary for the emancipation of their own class, or they are representatives of the petty bourgeoisie, a class which, until a democratic regime has been established and until the social measures necessitated by such a regime have been inaugurated, has many interests in common with the proletariat. At critical moments, therefore, the communists will have to make common cause with the democratic socialists, and temporarily at least to follow with them as much of a common policy as is possible. But they can do this only so long as these socialists do not enter the service of the ruling bourgeoisie and attack the communists. It is obvious, however, that such common action does not exclude the discussion of difference.

QUESTION 25: *What must be the attitude of the communists to the other political parties of our time?*

Answer: This attitude differs from country to country. In England, France and Belgium, where the bourgeoisie rules, the communists for the nonce still have interests in common with the various democratic parties. This community of interests is all the greater the more the democrats, in the socialistic measures they now advocate, approximate the aims of the communists; that is to say, the more clearly and definitely they represent proletarian interests, and rely upon the proletariat for support. In England, for instance, the Chartists, consisting of members of the working class, are incalculably nearer to the communists than are the democratically-minded petty bourgeois or so-called radicals.

In *America,* where the democratic constitution has been established, the communists must make common cause with the party that is utilizing this constitution in the interests of the proletariat and against the bourgeoisie, that is, with the agrarian National Reformers.

In *Switzerland* the Radicals, although they form a very mixed party are as yet the only people with whom the communists can cooperate. Among the Radicals, those in the cantons of Vaud and of Geneva are the most advanced.

In *Germany,* finally, the decisive struggle between the bourgeoisie and the absolute monarchy is still ahead. Since, however, the communists cannot enter upon the decisive struggle between them and the bourgeoisie until the latter has risen to power, it is in the interests of communism that the communists should help the bourgeoisie to attain that power as speedily as possible, and, subsequently, to overthrow that power as speedily as possible. Communists must, therefore, always rally to the support of the liberal bourgeois party in its struggle with the governments. But they must ever be on their guard least they should come to believe the self-deceptions of the bourgeois or their misleading assurances that its victory will in any way bring solace to the proletariat. The only advantages the communists will derive from a victory of the bourgeoisie will be: (1) various concessions which would render the communists' tasks of defending their principles and discussing and spreading their ideas less arduous, so that they could bring about the unification of the proletariat into a closely-knit, militant and organized class; and (2) the assurance that, from the day on which the absolute governments are overthrown, the war between the bourgeoisie and the proletarians will be on the order of the day. Henceforward, the party policy of the communists will be the same as that for communists in the countries where the bourgeoisie has already risen to power.

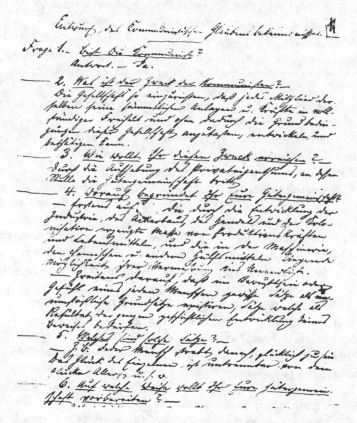

The opening of the manuscript of Engels' "Communist Confession of Faith."

III. DEMANDS OF THE COMMUNIST PARTY IN GERMANY

These demands were printed, in German, on a flyer in Paris about March 30, 1848, when the Executive Committee of the Communist League—or Communist Party as it called itself—resided in Paris. They were addressed to the thousands of German artisans working in that city who, excited by the revolution in Germany, were discussing ways and means of action.

1. The whole of Germany shall be declared a republic, one and indivisible.

2. Every German, having attained the age of 21, and provided he has not been a condemned criminal, shall be a voter and be eligible for election.

3. Representatives of the people shall be salaried so that manual workers, too, shall be able to become members of the German parliament.

4. Universal arming of the people. In future the armies shall be simultaneously worker-armies, so that the military arm shall not, as in the past, merely consume, but shall produce more than is actually necessary for its upkeep.

This will likewise be an aid to the organization of labor.

5. Legal services shall be free of charge.

6. All feudal dues, exactions, corvées, tithes, etc., which have hitherto pressed upon the rural population, shall be abolished without compensation.

7. Royal and other feudal domains, together with mines, pits, and so forth, shall become the property of the State. The domains shall be cultivated on a large scale and with the most up-to-date scientific devices in the interests of the whole of society.

8. Mortgages on peasant lands shall be declared the property of the State. Interest on such mortgages shall be paid by the peasant to the State.

9. In localities where the tenant system is developed, the land rent or the earnest money [*Pachtschilling*]* shall be paid to the State as a tax.

The measures advocated in Nos. 6, 7, 8 and 9 have been put forward with a view to decreasing the burdens hitherto imposed upon the peasantry and the small tenants without cutting down the means available for defraying State expenses and without imperilling production.

The landed proprietor who is neither a peasant nor a tenant, has no share in production. Consumption on his part is, therefore, pure abuse.

10. A State bank, whose paper issues are legal tender, shall replace all private banking concerns.

By this method credit can be regulated in the interest of the people *as a whole,* and thereby the dominion of the big financial magnates will be undermined. Further, by gradually substituting paper money for gold and silver coin, the means of exchange (that indispensable prerequisite of bourgeois trade and commerce) will be cheapened, and gold and silver will be set free for use in foreign trade. Finally, this measure is necessary in order to bind the interests of the conservative bourgeoisie to the cause of the revolution.

11. All the means of transport, railroads, canals, steamships, roads, the mails, etc. shall be taken over by the State. They shall become the property of the State and shall be placed free at the disposal of the impecunious classes.

12. Salaries of all civil servants shall be identical, except in the case where a civil servant has a family to support. His requirements being greater, his salary shall be higher.

13. Complete separation of Church and State. The clergy of every denomination shall be paid only by the voluntary contributions of their congregations.

* Money paid as a pledge to bind a bargain.

14. The right of inheritance to be curtailed.

15. The introduction of steeply graduated taxes, and the abolition of taxes on articles of consumption.

16. Inauguration of national workshops. The State guarantees a livelihood to all workers and provides for those who are incapacitated for work.

17. Universal and gratuitous popular education.

It is to the interest of the German proletariat, the petty bourgeoisie and the small peasantry to support these demands with all possible energy. Only by the realization of these demands will the millions in Germany, who have hitherto been exploited by a handful of persons and whom the exploiters would like to keep in further subjection, win the rights and attain to that power which they as the producers of all wealth are entitled to expect.

The Committee:

Karl Marx, Karl Schapper, H. Bauer, F. Engels, J. Moll, W. Wolff

IV. THE EARLY HISTORY OF THE MANIFESTO IN THE UNITED STATES

The *Manifesto* made its first appearance in America in the New York weekly, *Die Republik der Arbeiter,* October-November 1851.[1] Only Sections I and II appeared. Weitling was an editor of the paper and away on a tour; he probably suppressed further publication—at any rate, no more was published. Marx, in a letter to Weydemeyer, October 16, 1851, suggested that he might try to have the English translation published in Dana's *New York Tribune,* but nothing came of it. A later suggestion by Marx, in a letter to F. A. Sorge[2] in 1854, also came to nothing.

Interest in the *Manifesto* revived with the International Working Men's Association (IWA), better known as the First International. The *New York World* (September 21, 1871) published some parts of the English translation. Then a full English translation—the one by Macfarlane of 1850[3] with the Harney introduction—was published in *Woodhull and Claflin Weekly,* December 30, 1871. This was a periodical issued in New York by the two militant feminists, the sisters Virginia Woodhull and Tennessee Claflin, who also had run a medicine show and a stock brokerage office (under the auspices of Commodore Vanderbilt), and now dabbled in socialism.[4] They dominated Section 12 of the IWA, but were soon expelled because of their advocacy of free love. In this curious way the English version of the *Manifesto* arrived on the American scene.

From this version a French translation of Sections I and II was published between January and March 1872 in *Le Socialiste,* New York, the organ of the French section of the IWA. Engels was interested in the two translations and asked Sorge to send him copies. He needed especially the French version to counteract the propaganda of the Bakuninists and the Proudhonists in France.

Also in 1871 one of the Chicago sections of the IWA brought out, as a pamphlet, the original German text, after the second (Leipzig) edition of 1866. This was probably the edition which was recommended to Samuel Gompers, then a young cigarmaker in New York, by his friend Karl Laurrell, the secretary of the Scandinavian section of the IWA. Gompers later wrote in his autobiography:

" (Laurrell) placed in my hands a copy of the Communist Manifesto. As it was in German and my knowledge of the language was still inadequate, he translated and interpreted it for me paragraph by paragraph. That document brought me an interpretation of much that before had been inarticulate feeling.

"This insight into a hidden world of thought aroused me to master the German language in order that I might read for myself."[5]

There was a new wave of interest in the *Manifesto* in the 80's during the great struggles for the eight-hour day, in which the Chicago anarchists were very active. They published the German original as a pamphlet in 1883, and part of the old English translation appeared in *The Alarm* of February 1885, a paper published by Albert Parsons. After the Haymarket affair, the trial and execution of Parsons and his comrades, a part of this translation appeared in Parsons' book *Anarchism,* published in 1887 by Parsons' wife Lucy.

Then the Socialist Labor Party took over. The new English translation by Moore appeared in the *New York Workingmen's Advocate,* the organ of this party, in 1890; in the same year it appeared also as pamphlet. From now on it was regularly reprinted, in 1902 by C. H. Kerr in Chicago, the publishing house incorporated in 1893 and which in 1899 became associated with the Socialist Party. In the New York *Volkszeitung* of 1902, also an organ of the SLP, appeared a new German edition, and it was republished as a pamphlet.

The first publication of the English translation by the International Publishers was in 1930.

There have been several translations into other languages, for instance, a Czech edition in 1882 (New York) by the poet Leopold Kochman; Yiddish in 1897 in *Die Zukunft* (New York) by Abraham Kahan; Hungarian in 1916 (New York) and Yugoslav in 1926 (Chicago).

EXPLANATORY NOTES
AND INDEX

EXPLANATORY NOTES

The works by Marx and Engels, when possible, are quoted from existing English translations. Otherwise, quotations are translated by the editor from the *Marx-Engels Gesamtausgabe, Erste Abteilung* (7 vols., Frankfurt-Berlin, 1927–32), for short, *MEGA*. The works can also be consulted in Marx, Engels, *Werke* (39 vols. and 2 *Ergänzungsbände*, Berlin, 1955–68), which has the correspondence as well.

An excellent introduction to the period preceding the Revolution of 1848 can be found in E. L. Hobsbawm, *The Age of Revolution, 1789–1848* (New York, Toronto, 1962), with ample reference material. The best book available in English for the life of Marx and the development of the ideas of Marx and Engels in this period remains F. Mehring, *Karl Marx: The Story of His Life* (New York, 1935). The original German text was published in 1918, and therefore the author did not have available to him the many documents published since then, especially those from the formative period of Marx and Engels. Full use of these is made by A. Cornu, *Karl Marx et Friedrich Engels* (Paris, 3 vols, 1955–62), also in German. See also G. Mayer, *Friedrich Engels* (New York, 1969), first published in 1936.

Commentaries on the *Manifesto* and its origin exist in abundance, and from any possible angle. Among the best in English are Mehring, *Karl Marx* (see above) and D. Ryazanov, *The Communist Manifesto of Karl Marx and Friedrich Engels* (New York, International Publishers, 1930; reprint by Russell and Russell, New York, 1963), a translation from the Russian edition of 1922. Here again, it must be emphasized, both works are in some respect dated. This holds even more 'for the somewhat abstract commentary by A. Labriola, "In Memory of the Communist Manifesto," in *Essays on the Materialist Conception of History* (C. H. Kerr, Chicago, 1904; reprint by Monthly Review, 1966); the original Italian is from 1895.

Other commendable commentaries can be found in the chapter on the *Manifesto* in E. H. Carr, *Studies in Revolution* (London, 1950) and in the edition of the *Manifesto* by P. M. Sweezy and L. Huberman (New York, 1964). Useful for its historical account, but weak in some of its conclusions, is the commentary by H. Laski (first published London, 1948, latest edition by T. B. Bottomore, *H. J. Laski on the Communist Manifesto*. New York, 1967).

Among commentaries in other languages we recommend the account in *Geschichte der deutschen Arbeiterbewegung* I (Berlin, 1966) and the older one in F. Mehring, *Die Geschichte der deutschen Sozialdemokratie* (Stuttgart, 1897). An often reprinted French commentary, but very dated, is that by Ch. Andler, *Le manifeste communiste, introduction historique et commentaire* (Paris, 1901); the weaknesses have been pointed out by F. Mehring, *Neue Zeit* 20 (1901–02); also Mehring, *Gesammelte Schriften* (Berlin, 1963) pp. 215–28. Among more recent books on Marx and Engels available in English we can mention R. Garaudy, *Karl Marx, the Evolution of His Thought* (New York, 1967, from the French), and J. Lewis, *The Life and Teachings of Karl Marx* (New York and London, 1965).

INTRODUCTION

I.

1. *Neue Rheinische Zeitung,* Dec. 15, 1848, MEGA 7, p. 493 (all MEGA volumes cited are from *Erste Abteilung).*

2. A romantic view of Italy's rebellious youth is given by Ethel Boole Voynich in her novel *The Gadfly* (1897), more famous in the USSR than in her native England or in the United States.

3. This was no common informer, but the successful playwright August Kotzebue (1761–1819), whose works were collected in 40 volumes (1840–41). His plays, especially *The Stranger* and *Pizarro,* were performed on the English and American stage.

4. Among the English enthusiasts was Lord Byron, who organized a military expedition and died in Greece (1824). The Bostonian Samuel Gridley Howe went over as a naval surgeon and guerrilla fighter; after his return he founded Perkins School for the Blind in Boston. His wife Julia wrote "The Battle Hymn of the Republic."

5. On the early British labor movement see S. and B. Webb, *The History of Trade Unionism* (London, 1894, revised 1920). Also see E. P. Thompson, *The Making of the English Working Class* (New York, 1966); M. Beer, *A History of British Socialism* (2 vols., London 1919, 2nd ed. 1940). See also A. L. Morton, *A People's History of England* (Int. Publ., New York, new, revised ed., 1968; first ed., London, 1936).

6. *Mais quand notre règne arrive*
Quand votre règne finira
Alors nous tisserons le linceul du vieux monde
Car on entend déjà la révolte qui gronde . . .

7. *Hier im Ort ist ein Gericht*
Viel schlimmer als die Fehmen,
Wo man nicht mehr ein Urteil spricht
Das Leben schnell zu nehmen.

8. *Im düstern Auge keine Träne,*
Sie sitzen am Webstuhl und fletschen die Zähne,
"Deutschland, wir weben dein Leichentuch,
Wir weben hinein den dreifachen Fluch—
Wir weben, wir weben."

The English translation is by Engels, MEGA 4, p. 342.

II.

1. *Es erben sich Gesetz' und Rechte*
Wie eine ew'ge Krankheit fort;
Sie schleppen von Geschlecht sich zum Geschlechte,
Und rücken sacht von Ort zu Ort.
Verstand wird Unsinn, Wohltat Plage,
Weh dir, dasz Du ein Enkel bist!
Vom Rechte, das mit uns geboren ist
Von dem is leider nie die Frage.

2. *The Doctrine of Saint-Simon* (Boston, 1958); translated from *Doctrine de Saint-Simon. Exposition. Première année*, 1829, eds. C. Bougle, E. Halevy (Paris, 1924).

3. The terms socialism and communism appear in the 1820's and 1830's. Hobsbawm (see above) points out that a remarkable number of words belonging to our common vocabulary either date from this period or received in it their modern meaning. He mentions industry, factory, middle class, working class, capitalism, socialism, railway, liberal and conservative as political terms, nationality, scientist, engineer, proletariat and (economic) crisis. Also: utilitarian, statistics, sociology, journalism, ideology, strike (of workers) and pauperism. We may add communism, radicalism, biology and railroad (United States). Few of these words can be precisely dated, but scientist dates from 1840 (Whewell), technology from 1816 (J. Bigelow), anaesthesia from 1846 (O. W. Holmes). "To imagine the modern world without these terms," says Hobsbawm, "is to measure the profundity of the revolution which broke out between 1789 and 1848 and forms the greatest transformation in human history since the remote times when men invented agriculture and metallurgy, writing, the city and the state."

4. S. Bernstein, "Babeuf and Babouvism," *Science and Society* 2 (1937) pp. 29–57, 166–94; also: *Essays in Political and Intellectual History* (New York, 1955), Chapter V.

Babeuf's communism had predecessors throughout the ages. Of particular influence on Babeuf was the *Code de la Nature* by a certain

Morelly, of whom little is known except his books; in 1756 he was called *"ci-devant Régent à Vitry-le-Français."* The book, often ascribed to Diderot, appeared in 1755. It criticized the existing order sharply and projected an order according to nature with "no private property except objects of daily use." Every citizen should be occupied and maintained in behalf of society, so that he "will contribute for his part to the general weal according to his powers, his talents and his age." Marx knew the book in an 1841 edition (MEGA 5, p. 513). New edition with introduction by G. Chinard (1950, printed in Abbéville).

    5. MEGA 3, pp. 294–95; 6, p. 308.

    6. On Saint-Simon see Note 2, also F. E. Manuel, *The World of Henri Saint-Simon* (Cambridge, Mass., 1956), E. H. Carr, *op. cit.,* Ch. I, F. Engels, *Socialism, Utopian and Scientific* (Int. Pub., New York, 1935), the original German dates from 1885; G. D. H. Cole, *Socialist Thought, the Forerunners, 1789–1850* (London, 1953). The popular poet Béranger, who knew the aging Saint-Simon, wrote:

> *J'ai vu Saint-Simon le prophète,*
> *Riche d'abord, plus endetté,*
> *Qui des fondaments jusqu'au faîte,*
> *Refaisait la société.*

I saw Saint-Simon the prophet, First in wealth and then in debt, Who from foundations to the rooftop, Remade the social edifice.

    7. Béranger's story is that during the last ten years of his life Fourier used to be home at noon to await the man who was going to offer him the first million francs for his *phalanstère.* Although all *phalanstères* were short-lived, a modified type called *familistère* flourished for many years at the still existing stove and other hardware works of J. B. A. Godin (1817–88) at Guise in Northern France, totally reorganized in 1968. The best known Fourierist colony in the United States was Brook Farm, near Boston, home of transcendentalism (1845–47). Many outstanding literary figures were in some way connected with it, among them, Hawthorne, Margaret Fuller, Charles A. Dana. The latter was in 1849–62 an editor of the *New York Tribune,* in which function he engaged Marx to contribute articles. On Fourierism in the United States see P. S. Foner, *History of the Labor Movement in the United States,* I (New York, Int. Pub., 1947), pp. 174–80.

    8. See Note 2.

    9. On Proudhon (and Saint-Simon) see E. H. Carr, *op. cit.,* Ch. 3. Carr points out that Proudhon welcomed the *coup d'état* of December 2, 1851, which brought the man to power who in 1852 made himself the emperor Napoleon III. Compare this to Marx's *The Eighteenth Brumaire of Louis Bonaparte,* with its bitter denunciation of Napoleon. Proudhon was hostile to the North during the American Civil War.

10. See S. Bernstein, *Blanqui* (Paris, 1970). Eduard Bernstein, in his *Vorauszetzungen des Sozialismus* of 1899 (translated as *Evolutionary Socialism*, New York, 1911)—the book that attempted to give a theoretical foundation to revisionism—claimed that Marx and Engels in the period before and even after 1848 in their strategy were essentially Blanquists. This is wrong, as nobody has better pointed out than Lenin in October 1917 on the eve of the seizure of power: *Selected Works* VI (New York, Int. Pub., 1943) pp. 321–23.

11. Harney later told the story: "It was in 1843 that he [Engels] came over from Bradford to Leeds and enquired for me at *The Northern Star* office. A tall, handsome young man, with a countenance of almost boyish youthfulness, whose English, in spite of his German birth and education, was even then remarkable for its accuracy. He told me he was a constant reader of *The Northern Star* and took a keen interest in the Chartist movement. Thus began our friendship over fifty years ago" *(Reminiscenses of Marx and Engels,* Moscow *ca.* 1960, p. 192).

12. MEGA 4, pp. 457–71. On Harney see A. R. Schoyen, *The Chartist Challenge, a Portrait of G. J. Harney* (1958) and J. Saville, *The Red Republican* I (London, 1966).

13. The *Garantien* has been republished, with a preface by F. Mehring (Berlin, 1908); see also Mehring, *Gesammelte Werke* 4 (Berlin, 1963) pp. 85–126.

14. MEGA 4, p. 409.

15. On Weitling see C. Wittke, *The Utopian Communist* (Baton Rouge, 1950). On Weitling and the German revolutionary artisan movement from 1830–42 see W. Schieder, *Anfänge der deutschen Arbeiterbewegung* (Stuttgart, 1963).

16. See K. Obermann, *Joseph Weydemeyer* (New York, Int. Pub., 1947). Two other socialists are worth mentioning because of their relation to America, one a Frenchman, the other English. Etienne Cabet (1788–1856) was a lawyer, first a democratic politician, then after a visit to England during 1834–39, where he met Owen and read More's *Utopia,* the promotor of a peaceful transition to a communist society, which he described in *Voyage en Icarie* (1840)—Journey to Icaria. "Papa" Cabet tried to realize his Icaria in the United States, beginning in newly conquered Texas. For many years there were Icarian communities in the United States, one near Corning, Iowa, lasting until the end of the century.

The other was the American-born John Francis Bray (1809–97), who as a printer in Leeds wrote *Labour's Wrongs and Labour's Remedy* (1839, reprinted London, 1931), a keen indictment of capitalist society. The remedy, as he saw it, was in cooperative joint-stock companies to insure, eventually, community of property. Marx, in his *Poverty of Philosophy* (1847) discussed Bray's work with great respect, comparing it favorably to Proudhon's, but pointed out the futility of his remedy. Bray returned to the United States in 1842, and for many years played an active role in the Michigan labor movement. He died in Pontiac. See M. T. Jolliffe, *International Review for Social History*, 4 (1939) , pp. 1–38.

17. It is, of course, impossible to present even an outline of Hegel's system in a few words. The literature on him, already enormous, is likely to increase by leaps and bounds with the renewal of interest in Marx's philosophy. It is unfortunate that many commentaries on Hegel are even more difficult to understand than Hegel himself. Perhaps the simplest introduction in English is by H. Marcuse, *Reason and Revolution* (2nd ed., New York, 1954, paperback 1960). As Lenin has pointed out, Hegel's whole philosophy, and especially his method, dialectics, has to be studied thoroughly on the basis of modern knowledge and experience in the light of Marx's thought, and this process is only in its beginnings.

18. F. Engels, *Ludwig Feuerbach and the Outcome of Classical German Philosophy* (New York, Int. Pub., 1941; the original German text is from 1888).

19. Hess has recently been the subject of several extensive studies, partly due to the fact that he is considered a precursor of Zionism. His bones, interred in a Jewish cemetery in Germany, were a few years ago transferred to Israel. His *Philosophische und sozialistische Schriften 1837–1850* were published by A. Cornu and M. Mönke (Berlin, 1961). Recent Books: M. Mönke, *Neue Quellen zur Hess-Forschung*, Abhandlungen Deutsche Akademie der Wissenschaften 1964, no. 1.; E. Silberner, *Moses Hess. Geschichte seines Lebens* (Leiden, 1966).

20. Knowledge of French socialism came to Germany also through a book by Lorenz Stein, *Der Sozialismus und der Kommunismus des heutigen Frankreichs* (1842), the result of a semi-official study trip to France by a young man who later became Professor Lorenz von Stein, economist of Vienna.

21. MEGA 4, p. 409.

III.

1. *Economic and Political Manuscripts of 1844* (New York, Int. Pub., 1964).

2. See H. Selsam, H. Martel, *Reader in Marxist Philosophy* (New York, Int. Pub., 1963) pp. 53–60.

3. Michael Bakunin (1814–1876) of petty Russian nobility, left Russia in 1840 for Berlin and joined the young Hegelians. He became a socialist, a professional revolutionary, and collaborated on the *German-French Annals*. In 1844 he was in Paris where he met Marx and Proudhon; his contact with Proudhon strengthened his sympathies for

anarchism. During the Revolution of 1848 he took part in the street fighting in Prague and in Dresden. Taken prisoner, he spent ten years in Russian prisons. In 1861 he escaped; on his way back to Europe he visited Longfellow in Cambridge, Mass. In the First International he was the principal leader of the anarchists.

4. *The German Ideology* (Parts I and III, New York, Int. Pub., 1942). The full English text is in *The German Ideology* (Progress, Moscow, 1964).

5. In the preface to the *Contribution to the Critique of Political Economy* (1859), see Selsam, Martel, *op. cit.*, p. 186. See also Marx's letter to Annenkov at the head of this chapter.

6. MEGA 5, p. 34.

7. MEGA 5, p. 35, Selsam and Martel *op. cit.*, p. 199.

8. Selsam, Martel, *ibid.*, p. 318

9. *Wage-Labour and Capital* (New York, Int. Pub., 1933). This is an English translation of the German edition of 1891, prepared by Engels after Marx's death, "approximately as Marx would have written it in 1891."

10. *Deutsche Brüsseler Zeitung*, Jan. 23, 1848, MEGA 6, p. 389.

11. *Werke* 27 (1963), p. 61.

12. F. Engels, *Zur Geschichte des Bundes der Kommunisten* (see Appendix), preface to the 1885 edition of the *Enthüllungen über den Kommunistenprozess zu Köln* by Marx. Schapper was in the early fifties for a while estranged from Marx and Engels, but soon again became their loyal friend. In 1865 he became a member of the central committee of the First International. Bauer, in 1851, emigrated to Australia. Moll participated in the rebellion of 1849 in Baden and the Palatinate, and fell in battle.

13. Headquarters of the German Workers Educational Society were at 20 Great Windmill Street, near Piccadilly Circus, the building is probably that of the present Red Lion public house. Later the Society moved to 49 Tottenham Street, where it remained until 1902, after which it moved to 107 Charlotte Street in Soho. Among the groups that met here was the London Bolshevik organization whose secretary was Maxim Litvinov. Former USSR ambassador to England, Ivan Maisky, talks about it in his very readable reminiscenses. It was closed in 1918 after police raids. A German bomb destroyed it in 1940 (for some of these data I thank Mr. Andrew Rothstein).

14. MEGA 5, p. 471.

15. Marx also attacked Kriege for his excessive concessions to the American agricultural reform movement (see Note 1 to Section IV of the *Communist Manifesto,* and MEGA 6, pp. 10–13). Like Weitling Kriege returned for a while to Europe to participate in the German Revolution. He died shortly after his return to America. It was Kriege who invited Weitling to come to America. Both men misunderstood the anti-slavery movement and opposed the Abolitionists.

Another member of the Brussels group who landed in the United States, after having participated in the German Revolution, was Karl Heinzen (1809–80), who arrived in 1850, very bitter against Marx. He settled in Roxbury, Mass., and was engaged in propaganda for abolitionism among German workers, apart from being an active freethinker. He and Wendell Phillips were friends. See G. Wittke, *Against the Current* (Chicago, 1945).

16. The history of the League of the Just and its relation to the origin of the *Communist Manifesto* has been told by Marx and by Engels, whose accounts appear in this book. Marx and Engels wrote from memory and later research has given a much more detailed picture, also correcting these accounts on some points. See G. Schaepler, *Der Bund der Gerechten. Seine Tätigkeit in London 1840–1847*, Archiv für Sozialgeschichte (Hannover) 2 (1962) pp. 5–29. Also M. Nettlau, *Londoner deutsche kommunistische Diskussionen 1845*, Archiv für die Geschichte des Sozialismus und der Arbeiterbewegung (Grünberg's Archiv) 10 (1921–22) pp. 362–391; C. Grünberg, *Die Londoner kommunistische Zeitung und andere Urkunden aus dem Jahre* 1847. *Ibid.* 9 (1920–21) pp. 249–341; a short account in V. Adoratzky, *The History of the Communist Manifesto of Marx and Engels* (New York, Int. Pub., 1938).

17. B. Andréas, *Gründungsdokumente des Bundes der Kommunisten (Juni bis September 1847)*. (Hamburg, 1969).

18. The *Kommunistische Zeitung* has been reprinted in Grünberg, see note 16, translation as *Communist Journal* in the book by Ryazanov cited at the beginning of these notes, pp. 286–318. In a section of this *Journal* the editor attacks Cabet's scheme of colonization in the United States as harmful to the communist cause. Cabet had come to London and had tried in vain to win the Just to his cause: another sign of their growing sense of political realities.

19. Reprinted in Cornu-Mönke, see II, 19, pp. 359–68, 445–57.

20. The meeting took place at the quarters of the German Workers Educational Society, 20 Great Windmill St. (see Note 13), Marx, during his stay in London, also addressed a meeting of this society at the Whyte Hart Inn, Drury Lane (still standing).

21. F. Lessner, *Neue Zeit* 1 (1892–93), translated as "Before 1848 and After (Reminiscences of an Old Communist)" in *Reminiscences* (see II, 11) pp. 149–72.

22. 16 Liverpool Street.

IV.

1. *Karl Marx, an essay by H. J. Laski, with the Communist Manifesto* (New York, League for Industrial Democracy, 1933), p. 17. First published in London, 1921.

2. Karl Kautsky, *Das kommunistische Manifest ein Plagiat*, *Neue Zeit* 24 ii (1906) pp. 693–702.

3. Karl Marx. *The Communist Manifesto,* introduction by S. T. Possony (Chicago, 1954) p. xxxvi. Andler, in his essay on the *Manifesto* (cited at the head of these Notes), also stresses, it seems unduly, Marx's dependence on his predecessors, in this case again the French.

4. Lenin. *State and Revolution* (New York, Int. Pub., 1932), p. 29–30 (Chapter II, 3).

5. Wermuth, Stieber, *Die Communistische verschwörungen des neunzehnten Jahrhunderts* (2 vols, Berlin, 1853). Stieber was the chief prosecutor of the communists at the Cologne trial in 1852 and in his use of spies, perjurers, etc., set a now familiar example.

6. B. Andréas, *Le manifeste communiste de Marx et Engels, Histoire et bibliographie, 1848–1918* (Milano, Feltrinelli, 1963) has 429 pages of bibliography with comment.

7. Introduction to *The Class Struggles in France (1848–50),* Marx, Engels, *Selected Works* (New York, Int. Pub., 1968) pp. 654, 655.

8. Marx, *The Eighteenth Brumaire of Louis Bonaparte* (New York, Int. Pub., 1963), p. 19. This book, incidentally, was first published (in German) in the United States, in Weydemeyer's paper *Die Revolution* of 1852. "Here is Rhodus, leap here"—*Hic Rhodus, hic salta*—is an allusion to "The Braggart", one of Aesop's fables. It means: do not boast of what you may have done elsewhere, do it here! The Latin is from Erasmus, Hegel uses it in the introduction to his *Philosophy of Law.*

9. As a matter of fact, Marx and Engels could even be behind their time in their expectations. As late as January 23, 1847, Engels gave the king of Prussia time to 1849 to face the revolution. It came on March 18, 1848 (MEGA 6, p. 391).

10. Preface to the Russian translations of *Letters by J. F. Becker,* etc. (1907), in Lenin, *Marx, Engels, Marxism* (Moscow, 1951) p. 231.

11. Marx, Lenin, *Civil War in France: Paris Commune* (New York, Int. Pub. 1968), pp. 54–55.

12. Marx, *Critique of the Gotha Programme,* (New York, Int. Pub., 1938), pp. 18, 8, 9, 10.

13. On this also see the edition of the *Communist Manifesto,* P. N. Sweezy and L. Huberman, eds. (New York, 1964) pp. 91–96.

14. MEGA 5, p. 50.

15. MEGA 6, 360–61. Marx and Engels were in London as delegates to the second congress of the Communist League.

16. MEGA 4, p. 457.

17. In the resolution written by Marx on the relations between the Irish and the British working class, accepted by the Council of the First International on Jan. 1, 1870: *Werke* 16, pp. 409–20, translation in K. Marx, *Letters to Kugelmann* (London, 1935), see p. 108. See also H. Davis, Note 21 below, p. 66.

18. MEGA 6, p. 652.

19. MEGA 6, p. 396.

20. F. Engels, *The Role of Force in History* (Int. Pub., New York, 1968), the original was written in 1887–88: *Werke* 21, p. 405.

21. See further H. Davis, *Nationalism and Socialism* (New York, 1967), a study of the position of Marx, Engels, Lenin and other Marxist authors on nationalism up to 1917. Those who read Dutch can find another account (to *ca.* 1935) from a Marxist point of view in A. S. De Leeuw, *Het socialisme en de natie* (Amsterdam, 1939).

22. See, e.g., *The Communist Manifesto*, S. H. Beer, ed. (New York, 1955). Professor Beer, after having noted "the extreme economic determinism of the Marxist theory," later (p. xxi) discovers that Marx "clearly departs from this strict version of economic determinism." Even Marx, clever though he was, was unable to depart from a position he never held.

23. *Capital* I, Chapter 3, Sect. 2: "The Metamorphosis of Commodities."

V.

1. *Kein offner Hieb in offner Schlacht*
   Es fällen die Nücken and Tücken
   Es fällt mich die schleichende Niedertracht
   Der schmutzigen Westkalmücken!

2. This trial, held from October 4 to November 12, 1852, at a time when Prussian reaction had recovered its courage, set the pattern for many anti-communist trials to follow in its use of intimidation, informers, police legends, falsification of documents, etc. There were eleven defendants (the twelfth defendant, the poet Freiligrath, was in London). Three of them got six, three five years of prison, one (Lessner) one year. All defendants had already been in jail for more than a year.

One of the defendants (acquitted) was the physician Dr. Abraham Jacobi (1832–1919). He emigrated to the United States, where he entered upon a very distinguished medical career, pioneering in the field of children's diseases. See R. Truax, *The Doctors Jacobi* (Boston, 1952).

MANIFESTO OF THE COMMUNIST PARTY

I.

1. Engels, *The Origin of the Family, Private Property and the State* (New York, Int. Pub., 1942).

2. Subsequently Marx pointed out that the worker does not sell his labor but his labor power, and used the more exact terms, the "value of labor power," and the "price of labor power." See, e.g., Engels' introduction to Marx's *Wage-Labour and Capital,* and Note 9 to Section III, Introduction.

II.

1. The measures here proposed are not necessarily those to which Marx and Engels gave top priority. They were probably those that resulted from the London congress of June and December 1847 where the Communist League was founded. They differ somewhat from the demands laid down in the Paris statement of March 1848 signed by Marx, Engels, Wolff, Schapper, Bauer and Moll. These are particularly directed toward Germany and represent more accurately what Marx and Engels considered most important. See also the commentaries in the books by Andler and Ryazanov.

2. This demand was widely held by socialists and communists of all shades, including Chartists. In his address to the Central Council of the Communist League in March 1850 Marx wrote that when feudalism is abolished, "the confiscated property must remain in the hands of the state and be converted into worker colonies cultivated by the associated rural proletariat with all the advantages of large scale agriculture. In this way the principle of common property will immediately obtain in a firm basis in the midst of the unstable bourgeois property relations." It is clear that none of the demands asks for nationalization of bourgeois property, since Marx and Engels, in 1848–50, supported the demands of the bourgeoisie in its fight against feudalism as a prerequisite for the proletarian revolution. Marx refers to this demand in his letter of June 20, 1881 to F. A. Sorge, in which he states his position on the book of Henry George *Progress and Poverty* (1880). See Note 1 to Section IV of the *Communist Manifesto.*

3. William Pitt, as British Prime Minister, had introduced in 1798 an income tax—then a novelty, not only in England—as a temporary measure to defray the cost of the war against France. It was repealed in 1815 and the documents were burned. The Prime Minister Robert Peel, in 1842, revived the income tax because of the increase in the national debt. Sharp demands that it be graduated as to income were voiced by Chartists. See Marx on taxes and national debt, *Capital,* vol. i, Ch. XXI. A comic note is struck by some reactionaries today who fight the income tax because it is a demand of the *Communist Manifesto.* They should blame Pitt and Peel.

4. A special demand of the Saint-Simonians.

5. This demand came out of the French Revolution and was also voiced by Babeuf.

6. A demand stressed by the Saint-Simonians and other French socialists who believed in state assistance for their reforms. This demand was often based on utopian schemes, and Marx had attacked Proudhon sharply on his bank scheme. From Engels' explanation in his *Principles of Communism* it appears that for him and Marx the demand was based on the conviction that the bourgeois revolution would be quickly followed by the proletarian one, so that the working class would already have a centralized credit system. (It will be remembered that in the United States the Jeffersonians fought *against* the centralization of the banking system.)

7. See Note 2. A comic note is struck by one recent commentator (Possony, see Note 3, Section IV, Introduction) who sees this demand as "the proposed introduction of slave labor."

8. On this point, which Marx and Engels always considered of grave importance, see Engels, *Anti-Dühring*, Part III, Chap. iii.

9. Free education was a demand voiced already by Babeuf and is recurrent in socialist writings such as those of Owen and Fourier. The combination of education with industrial production was also one of those demands which Marx and Engels always considered of great importance; see, for instance, *Capital* vol. I, Part iv, Section 9 on "The Factory Acts."

III.

1. The Legitimists were the adherents of the ancient nobility and their retainers who advocated the restoration of the Bourbon dynasty, overthrown in 1830, in the person of the grandson of Charles X.

2. "Young England," a group of British conservatives, many of them younger members of the aristocracy, formed about 1844. Their ideal was a regenerated feudalism, where "each knew his place—king, peasant, peer or priest—the greatest owned connection with the least," in the words of Lord John Manners in his poem "England's Trust" (1841). Benjamin Disraeli, later Prime Minister, was one of the group. Thomas Carlyle shared many of their ideas. In their favor it must be said that many of them were active in behalf of social legislation.

3. We think of Lamennais and the Christian socialists in England, see Sect. II, 2 of the Introduction.

4. Jean Charles Leonard Simonde de Sismondi (1773–1842), Swiss economist and historian, exposed in his *Nouveaux principes d'économie politique* (1818) the fundamental contradictions of capitalism: unlimited expansion of productive power accompanied by reducing the mass of producers to the merest subsistence level. In his search for a remedy he never advanced beyond the position of the small proprietor. One of his admirers, J. P. Villeneuve-Bargemont, a Catholic nobleman, wrote *Economie politique chrétienne* (3 vols., 1834).

5. Reference is to Kant's *Critique of Practical Reason* (1788).

6. The *Réformistes* were those who shared the opinions of the newspaper *La Réforme,* published in Paris from 1843 to 1850. The paper was radical republican and had connections with socialists. The editor, Ferdinand Flocon (1800–60), invited Marx to Paris in March 1848, when he was, with Louis Blanc, a member of the new provisional government. The *Réformistes* also called themselves social democrats. See also the note by Engels to the next section.

IV.

1. The Agrarians or National Reformers were a group in the United States, led by English-born George Henri Evans, a pupil of Owen. Starting about 1840, they agitated for free land: every citizen should have the right to a portion of the public domain. Free land in the West would free workers from dependence on capital, advance wages in the East and restore economic independence to the workers now crushed by the industrial revolution. There was a fair amount of utopianism in this movement, as Marx pointed out in his critique of Kriege (see Note 15 to Section III of Introduction). The Agrarian Reformers were behind the anti-rent movements of farmers in the backlands of Albany, New York. See Foner, *History of the Labor Movement in the United States,* vol. I, pp. 183–88, and H. Christman, *Tin Horns and Calico* (New York, 1945). The single tax movement, originating with Henry George (1839–97) and still existing, is a descendant of this agrarian reform activity.

2. Louis Blanc (1811–82), French historian and politician, who belonged to the *La Réforme* group (see above). He advocated state socialism, including social workshops where workers would receive work by and for the state. In order to appease him and his followers the revolutionary government in 1848 instituted *ateliers nationaux,* which were a failure.

3. Switzerland was governed by aristocratic elements, against which there was constant opposition by the democrats. This led to civil strife, as in the Sonderbund war of 1846. A democratic revolution occurred in Geneva in 1846, in which a radical party, consisting of different political elements, played a role.

4. The Polish Democratic Society, founded in 1832, appealed to the peasants against the aristocrats, and was supported by many Polish exiles. It organized the uprising of 1846 in Cracow. Its leader was Ludwik Mieroslavski (1814–78), active in all Polish uprisings from 1830 to 1863. He was honored (while imprisoned in Berlin) at the London meeting of November 29, 1847, addressed by Marx, Engels, Harney and Jones.

PREFACES BY MARX AND ENGELS

GERMAN EDITION OF 1872

1. The *Red Republican* was published by Harney between June and November 1850. Helen Macfarlane was one of his collaborators, "the only one of them who had real ideas—a *rara avis* [rare bird] in his little paper," wrote Marx to Engels, Feb. 23, 1851. We know little of her except that she lived at Burnley, not far from Manchester, and was a friend of Marx, Engels and Harney. If she was the same person who wrote under the name of Howard Mortin in left-wing Chartist papers, then she was well read and widely traveled, and inclined toward the Christian revolutionary tradition of Lamennais. She wrote of "sansculotte Jesus." See the reproduction of *The Red Republican*, J. Saville (London, 1966), p. xii. Her translation of the *Manifesto* was introduced by Harney who here revealed for the first time that the authors were "Citizens Charles Marx and Frederic Engels." The translation has its peculiarities; it opens with the statement that "a frightful hobgoblin stalks throughout Europe," and for "petty-bourgeois socialism" it coins the term "shopocrat socialism."

2. *Le Socialiste* was the organ of the French section of the First International in the United States, founded in 1870 in New York. It published the *Manifeste de Karl Marx* during January-March 1872. It was translated from the shortened English translation that appeared in *The Woodhull and Claflin's Weekly* of Dec. 30, 1871 (without mention of the names of the authors).

3. This first Russian translation of 1869 was by Bakunin, at that time residing in Switzerland. Some inadequacies in the translation were removed by G. V. Plekhanov in a new translation of 1882, also in Geneva, with a preface by Plekhanov; see *Neue Zeit* 26 (1908) p. 837.

4. Marx, Lenin, *Civil War in France: Paris Commune* (New York, Int. Pub., 1968), p. 54.

RUSSIAN EDITION OF 1882

1. See Note 3 above. The *Kolokol* (Bell) was published by the great Russian democrat Alexander Herzen, from 1856 to his death in 1870.

2. The Tsar's palace in Gatchina, now Krasnoarmeisk, 28 miles southwest of Leningrad, now a museum.

3. Village commune.

GERMAN EDITION OF 1883

1. This edition was published in 1883 as the "authorized third German edition," in Switzerland. It could not appear in Germany because of Bismarck's anti-socialist law of 1878.

English Edition of 1888

1. This is the English edition now in regular use and also used in this book. It was prepared, under Engels' direction, by Samuel Moore *(ca.* 1830–1911), a lawyer, friend of Marx and Engels, member of the First International. With Edward Aveling he also translated *Capital,* vol. I into English. The English edition of the *Manifesto* differs in some minor respects from the original German; for these differences see MEGA 6, p. 605. There also exists a translation by E. and C. Paul, made in 1928 and used in Ryazanov's book (see remarks at head of these Notes).

2. Ferdinand Lassalle (1825–64) was the founder, in 1863, of the General German Workers Union, a precursor of the German Social-Democratic Party.

3. The Bakunin translation was in 1869, not 1863. The translation of 1882 was by Plekhanov, as Engels himself later pointed out. Vera Zasulich, or Sassulich (1851–1919), was an active member first of the Narodnik, later of the Social-Democratic movement in Russia.

German Edition of 1890

1. This edition appeared in London as "fourth authorized German edition." In the same year Bismarck's anti-socialist law was repealed.

Polish Edition of 1892

1. The first Polish translation appeared in 1848. Engels sent his preface to the Polish socialist Stanislaw Mendelson (1857–1913) then in London (Feb. 11, 1892).

Italian Edition of 1893

1. The translator was Pasquale Martignetti (1844–1920), an Italian socialist who translated several works of Marx and Engels. It appeared first in the periodical *Lotta de classe,* Sept.–Dec. 1892.

MARX AND ENGELS ON THE HISTORY OF THE COMMUNIST LEAGUE

1. Marx-Engels, *Werke,* 14 (Berlin, Dietz, 1964), pp. 438–39. English translation by the editor.

2. *Ibid.,* 8 (Berlin, 1960), pp. 577–86. Engels' introduction can be found *ibid,* 21 (1962), pp. 206–16.

3. As we have seen, there were two congresses. The latter one, here mentioned, lasted ten days.

4. This translation is based on that by E. and C. Paul, in Ryazanov's book (cited at head of these Notes). Some changes have been made to bring it more in conformity with our text.

5. Jakobus Venedey (1805–71), radical publicist and politician, anticommunist, later a liberal.

6. Georg Büchner (1813–37), German poet, still known for his play *Danton's Tod* (Danton's Death). His attempt in 1832 to start a peasants' rebellion in Hesse failed before it got under way. Büchner fled to Switzerland. The Frankfurt affair was an unsuccessful *putsch* by a group of 50 radicals, mostly students. Mazzini's attempt in 1834 to invade Savoy from Switzerland with a small army of partisans failed after a few days. Mehring argues, *Gesammelte Schriften* 4 (Berlin, 1963) p. 274, that Engels was mistaken on Schapper's participation in Büchner's and Mazzini's adventures.

7. August Becker (1814–71), the "Red Becker," guiding spirit of the Swiss communist artisans after Weitling's arrest in 1843; wrote articles and pamphlets. Like some present-day rebels he affected a picturesque figure: long red beard, vest without coat, black beret, high boots, a big club in his hand; poor as a church mouse, he traveled around preaching rebellion. He later emigrated to the United States. He should not be confused with Johann Philip Becker (1809–86), a Swiss comrade of Marx and Engels in the First International.

8. Christian Friedrich Mentel (*b. ca* 1820), tailor from Potsdam, member of the Just in London and Paris, then in Berlin. He turned informer after a police raid in spring 1847. Later he emigrated to America. His information seems to have led to persecution among the Germans in Paris (see Andréas, Sect. III of Introduction, Note 17, p. 37). Alexander Beck was a tailor in Magdeburg.

9. This was, it seems, primarily due to the founding of the Fraternal Democrats in 1845.

10. This was the *Association démocratique,* founded in Brussels during the fall of 1847. It took after the London Fraternal Democrats and united proletarian rebels, most of them German, with progressive bourgeois and petty-bourgeois democrats.

11. August Hermann Ewerbeck (Engels writes "Everbeck") (1816–60), physician from Danzig; joined the Paris section of the Communist League. He translated Cabet's *Icarie* into German.

12. This was the work of the Communist Correspondence Committee.

13. Harro Paul Harring (1798–1880), Danish-born adventurer in revolutionary schemes from Poland to Argentina. A Hollywood type of "hero," he spread confusion wherever he went. On Kriege, see Sect. III of Introduction. Marx raked him over the coals in his "Great Men of the Exile," *Werke* 8 (1960) pp. 292–98.

14. Karl Albrecht (1788–1844), a merchant who, as the "prophet," preached his brand of confused religious-mystical socialism throughout Switzerland. Georg Kuhlmann (b. 1812) from Holstein, studied at Heidelberg, preached "true" socialism; also Metternich agent; *The German Ideology* has a section on him.

15. Karl Pfänder (1818–1876), member of the Communist League and later of the General Council of the First International. Johann Georg Eccarius (1818–89), tailor from Tübingen, member of the Communist League, became general secretary of the First International. Friedrich Lessner (1823–91), tailor from Weimar, one of the defendants in the Cologne trial of 1852. Lessner was condemned to three years in prison, later emigrated to London, where he was on the executive council of the First International. Late in life he wrote *Reminiscences of Marx and Engels* (see Introduction, Section II, Note 11 and Section III, Note 21). Georg Lochner *(ca.* 1824–after 1871) was a carpenter, friend of Marx and Engels in London.

16. This article was only adopted at the second congress of the League.

17. See Introduction, Section IV, Note 5. In Andréas' book (III, Note 17) Engels' account of the statutes is supplemented and corrected with more details.

THE COMMUNIST CREDOS BY ENGELS

1. The "Draft of the Communist Confession of Faith" was found, together with four other documents pertaining to the first congress of the Communist League, among the papers of Joachim Friedrich Martens in the manuscript collection of the Staats- und Universitäts-bibliothek in Hamburg, Germany, in 1968. They were published by B. Andréas (see Note 17, Section III, Introduction). See also review by E. Bottigelli, *"Aux origines de la ligue des communistes,"* *Mouvement Social* (Paris, 1970), pp. 139–42. English translation of the draft is by Ruth Struik.

Martens (1806–77) was one of those roving artisans typical of the time, a Hamburg man who joined the League of the Just in Paris and later moved back to Hamburg. Here he was a founder of the local Workers Educational Society and a member of the local section of the Just. His papers were deposited with the Staatsbibliothek in 1912.

This June "Confession of Faith" had been preceded by another draft, issued by the Executive Committee of the League of the Just, a part in November 1846 and another in February 1847, showing how Schapper and his friends were struggling for clarification of their position at the time they were approaching Marx and Engels. There are seven questions and answers. Example: *"Question* 1: What is communism and what do the communists want? *Answer:* Communism is a system according to which the earth should be common property of man, everyone should work according to his faculties, and everyone should enjoy himself, 'consume' according to his capacities. The communists therefore intend to abolish the whole social order and institute a completely new one in its stead."

Question 5 discusses the position of the proletariat with respect to the "higher and lower bourgeoisie"; Question 6, that with respect to religious parties; Question 7, that with respect to the social and communist parties. The answer to this last question ends with, "A serious, serene, attitude compels the tyrants to take off their masks, and then victory or death!" See *C. Grünberg,* (III, Note 16), pp. 330–33.

2. "Principles of Communism" was found among the posthumous papers of Engels and was published for the first time by E. Bernstein in the Berlin *Vorwärts* in 1914. The translation here is based on the rendition by E. and C. Paul, appearing in Ryazanov's edition of the *Communist Manifesto* (cited at the head of these notes), pp. 319–40, which the editor checked and revised according to the German text in MEGA 6, pp. 503–22. Other English translations are by M. Bedacht (Chicago, *ca.* 1925), G. Baracchi (Melbourne, Australia, 1933) and P. M. Sweezy (New York, 1952).

3. Heide was Wilhelm Wolff, Schill was Schapper.

4. This question is answered in the June draft, Question 12.

5. Marx, in the *Communist Manifesto,* is far less categorical than Engels concerning the simultaneity of the communist revolution "in all civilized countries."

6. This description of communist society is perhaps the most explicit Engels (and Marx) ever gave, although they returned to several of the points Engels made in the course of their later writing. Marx, in his *Critique of the Gotha Program* (1875), gave a necessary complementation.

7. These questions are answered in the June draft (Questions 12, 21 and 22).

THE EARLY HISTORY OF THE MANIFESTO IN THE
UNITED STATES

1. Most of this material is taken from Andréas, see Sect. IV of Introduction, Note 6.

2. Frederick Adolph Sorge (1828–1906), close friend and associate of Marx and Engels; organizer of Sections of the First International in the United States, and Secretary of the General Council of the First International after it was transferred to New York (1872–74).

3. See Note 1 to the German edition of the *Manifesto* of 1872.

4. On the Claflin sisters see E. Sachs, *The Terrible Siren, Victoria Woodhull* (1838–1927), (New York, 1928).

5. S. Gompers, *Seventy Years of Life and Labor* (New York, 1957), p. 74.

Index